Institute
for
Policy Studies

South Africa:

Foreign Investment and Apartheid

Lawrence Litvak,
Robert DeGrasse &
Kathleen McTigue

The Institute for Policy Studies is a non-partisan research institute. The views expressed in this study are solely those of the author.

© 1978 Institute for Policy Studies

Editor: Helen Hopps

Copies of this book are available from the Institute for Policy Studies, 1901 Q Street, N.W., Washington, D.C. 20009 or Paulus Potterstraat 20, 1071 DA, Amsterdam, Holland.

Second Printing: 1979
First Printing: 1978
ISBN 0-89758-009-5

C-417

In Memory
of
Steve Biko

The authors of this book are members of the SOUTH AFRICA CATALYST PROJECT.

The SOUTH AFRICA CATALYST PROJECT was formed in June 1977 by twenty Stanford community members involved in the Stanford Committee for a Responsible Investment Policy (SCRIP). It was created in response to requests from college activists interested in changing American foreign policy and ending university investments in South Africa. The Project has produced an organizer's handbook and sponsored a full-time traveller to distribute information on the role of U.S. investment in South Africa and catalyze activity on California campuses. Another collective has since been formed in the Northeast. The Catalyst Project provides support and information on alternative investments and current anti-apartheid activity to a growing campus network.

The South Africa Catalyst Project has been funded by:
    Agape Foundation
    Vanguard Foundation
    Limantour Fund
    People's Life Fund

Contents

Foreword

As the political and moral attack on the government of South Africa grows stronger—both from within by the African liberation movement, and from without—the defenders of the status quo retreat to more "liberal" positions. Once upon a time, it was enough to justify oppression of the African majority in South Africa by speaking of the civilizing impact of white rule.

When the era of independence came to Africa, this argument was no longer tenable. The defenders of the status quo retreated to discussing the dangerous nature of extremist African movements. But as the movements demonstrated their strength and political maturity, new defenses were sought.

The favorite one today is to agree that change is inevitable, but that only slow change will work. And what kind of slow change is advocated? Astonishingly, it is argued that strengthening the economic basis of the white *apartheid* regime will in fact bring change. This is nonsense, and those who speak it know it. The authors of this pamphlet lay out the evidence with great clarity. Continued American investment in South Africa *in any form* is continued American support for the oppressive regime in power.

Those who wish to support change in South Africa have only two ways to do it: (1) active assistance to the liberation movement; (2) a call for United States economic disinvestment and political disengagement from the present South Africa state. The rest is sophistry.

Professor Immanuel Wallerstein,

State University of New York at Binghamton
Co-Chairman, Association of Concerned African Scholars

Introduction

The winds of change are blowing across the African continent. Mozambique and Angola, important buffer states separating the white minority regimes of South Africa and Rhodesia from black Africa, were liberated in 1975. School children in Soweto Township defied the South African regime's authority during June 1976 in the largest black protest since the Sharpville massacre of 1960. Steve Biko's death last fall, while imprisoned by apartheid officials, caused massive outcry, both within South Africa and throughout the international community. The white regime brutally repressed these protests, yet blacks continue to demand self-determination.

Steve Biko's Black Consciousness Movement, a central force encouraging black resistance, asserts simply that all people, regardless of skin color, deserve equal respect. This booklet examines United States involvement in South Africa from the perspective that meaningful change must bring equal political and economic participation, with majority rule and protection of individual rights, to all people living in South Africa. Anything less will not suffice.

We challenge those who assert U.S. involvement in South Africa liberalizes apartheid. Labor practices of U.S. corporations differ little from other foreign and domestic corporations. Denying black people political rights historically has been the basis for South African economic growth. Economic prosperity provides apartheid officials with greater resources for repression. American investors only reinforce and legitimate these realities by remaining in South Africa.

While U.S. corporations do not threaten the status quo, they clearly contribute economic support to apartheid. IBM supplies computers which help administer the prison system. U.S. oil firms supply 44% of South Africa's crude. U.S. banks provide one-third of all loans. GM and Ford build vehicles used by the minority regime's defense forces. In times of danger, U.S. firms are required by law to furnish the regime with strategic products.

Economic sanctions against the minority regime, including corporate withdrawal, will most quickly pave the way toward full political participation by all races in South Africa. While ultimately the people of South Africa shape their own liberation, without continued investment, loans and trade, it would be far more difficult for South African whites to finance the current level of repression. For over fifteen years the United States government has condemned apartheid. During the same period, U.S. corporate investment has increased four times and return on investment has consistently outdistanced the worldwide average. Yet South Africa has not modified the institutional racism upon which apartheid exists.

We believe pressure for change and support for black resistance must grow. A U.S. economic boycott would support black efforts to transform apartheid by encouraging consessions from the South African regime. Concessions provide greater resources for black resistance, a critial role because white repression and black poverty drastically limit protest. The black school children who faced police guns in Soweto were not asking for integrated bathrooms, they were demanding the right to shape their own future.

While this report is relatively technical we have tried to avoid overburdening the reader with statistics. A good source of statistics on black conditions in South Africa is the UN publication *Basic Facts on the Republic of South Africa and the Policy of Apartheid.* Anyone interested in further study should consult it as well as the sources listed in our reference section.

This report, a product of the South Africa Catalyst Project, is a collective effort, but we feel a special note should be made of the contribution of Larry Litvak. He is responsible for the research of the Catalyst Project and put a tremendous amount of his considerable abilities into this analysis.

RD

SOUTH AFRICA CATALYST PROJECT
570 Oxford St., No. E
Palo Alto, California 94306

Note on usage: The South African Rand is roughly equivalent to $1.15 U.S. In this booklet "black" refers to African. "Non-white" refers to all people of color.

I.
The Progressive Force Argument: A Critical Appraisal

The most widely held and frequently voiced justification for continued American investment in South Africa has been the so-called "progressive force" argument. The heart of the progressive force position is the notion that the economic growth accompanying continued investment will inevitably undermine and destroy the system of apartheid. It is assumed that as investment and GNP rise, so must the incomes and job status of black South Africans. Upgrading Africans' standard of living and security in the labor market will eventually lead to their full and equal integration into society on all levels, political and social as well as economic. Apartheid will bow because its goal of black disenfranchisement is simply incompatible with further capitalist growth in the country.[1]

South Africa's leading business weekly, the Johannesburg *Financial Mail* has summed up the argument:

> Every extra rand invested is thus another ray of hope for those trapped on the dark side of apartheid, every extra job created is another step toward the peaceful transition that the inexorable process of economic life will impose. And, as African living standards improve, as they become more educated, as the cultural gap closes, and as their way of life moves close to that of Western society, so it is hoped that the fear which explains so much that is otherwise inexplicable in this country, will subside and a realization of the true complementarity of the White and Black increasingly take its place.[2]

Since the 1940's, this position has been reiterated by both South African and foreign business people. It was first expressed in an organized political fashion inside South Africa with the creation of the Progressive Party in 1959. Harry Oppenheimer, a founding member of the party and chairman of the giant Anglo-American Corporation, has been its most enthusiastic proponent.[3]

The impetus foreign capital is said to lend to this progressive force has been increasingly emphasized in recent years, often by U.S. corporations responding to criticism of their South African operations. For example, in

11

a 1973 publication concerning its South African subsidiary, Ford Motor Company argued:

> Ford believes that the industrialization of South Africa is bringing social and economic changes that will increasingly benefit all groups in that nation, and that the presence of American-owned companies in South Africa is a positive factor in encouraging economic progress and equal opportunity.[4]

Investors like Ford maintain that they are in a position to demonstrate the superiority of more enlightened and non-discriminatory labor practices.

While the progressive force argument stands as an attractive position for those attempting to both engage in investment in South Africa and express opposition to racism there, it is a position resting upon shaky foundations. It is an essentially incorrect account of the relationship between economic growth and racial oppression in South Africa. Rather than acting as a liberalizing influence, economic growth has been accompanied by intensified repression of the black populace. Rather than serving as a constraint on industrialization and economic growth, apartheid has been a sophisticated mechanism for regulating a flow of cheap black labor upon which the dynamism of South African capitalism has been based. Rather than weakening apartheid, foreign investment has reinforced it.

The basic assumptions of the progressive force argument and a critique of them follow. In challenging each set of assumptions, a more accurate picture of present-day realities in South Africa will emerge, as well as a critical evaluation of the true prospects for change associated with continued American investment.

Historical Roots of Racial Oppression in South Africa

Much of the progressive force belief that apartheid can be modernized out of existence stems from assumptions about the historical roots of present-day racial oppression in South Africa. Typically two factors are singled out as primarily accounting for the development and persistence of discrimination against non-whites in the country.

The first of these explanatory factors is pure race prejudice. It is said that the origins of the prejudice extend back to the first period of contact between the black and white races in South Africa. It has been compared to the race prejudice traditionally prevalent in the southern United States, also historically based on the master/slave relationship of the first interaction between whites and blacks. This race prejudice is regarded as essentially irrational but preserved by the unusual degree of Afrikaner cultural and social exclusiveness.

The second explanatory factor is the desire of the white working class in South Africa to gain and protect a privileged position in the labor market. This is considered to be more rational than race prejudice. Should job and wage discrimination be eliminated, it is argued, the living standards of working whites would be adversely affected. The economic interests which apartheid could possibly serve are thus seen to be those of white employees rather than owners of capital.

In emphasizing racial ideology and the entrenchment of the white working class as basic causes of black oppression, the progressive force argument posits a social system in South Africa that could be significantly transformed by industrialization and economic growth. But this set of assumptions about the roots of racial domination in South Africa ignores what is in many ways a more fundamental force in the history of the country: the development of an economy based on cheap and powerless African labor. Looking at this dimension of South African history reveals a great deal of consistency between economic development and the disenfranchisement of blacks.

There is substantial evidence for the view that race relations in South Africa have in large part consisted of the imposition of newer and more refined methods for forcing blacks to labor at a cheap wage. Much of this evidence can be found in the extent to which laws and policies which institutionalize white power and black powerlessness have been out-growths of the economy's changing labor requirements.[5]

Exploitation of black South Africans in white economic enterprise dates back to the arrival and early settlement of Europeans in South Africa, beginning in the latter half of the 17th century. Having established a staging post for India-bound vessels in 1652, the Dutch East India Company required a supply of meat to provision crews for their long voyage ahead. Both cattle and land were taken from the San and Khoi peoples, despite their resistance. Jan van Riebeeck, the Dutch commander, defended the conquest of this stock by stating that it "... now had become the property of the Company by the sword and the laws of war."[6] His remark signalled the beginning of a crucial theme which has woven its way through South African history: non-whites and their economic resources can be exploited to their fullest through coercion—sometimes subtle but more often overt.

As white immigration to South Africa increased throughout the first half of the 19th century, a class of Dutch farmers (the Boers) emerged and gradually moved inland in search of both additional land and independence from the growing mercantile-oriented British interests on the Cape. Major clashes between the advancing Boers and· Africans attempting to stop the encroachment ensued. Employing a superior technology of guns, horses and wagons, the Boers prevailed. For several decades after the Kaffir (African) war began in 1779, this pattern of Boer expansion repeated itself, the most famous instance being the Great Trek. While many African crops and cattle were destroyed during this period,

13

and much land was expropriated, there was no effort at systematically channeling black labor into the European economy, which was almost wholly agrarian.[7] The commercial enterprises that did exist, producing wine, wool and sugar for export, relied almost entirely on imported slaves and indentured labor.

Some exceptions to this general situation existed, and these fore-shadowed important changes to come.[8] On the Cape, the Khoi people had been made landless early on; having miscegenated to a large extent with imported slaves newly freed by the British, they became the Cape Coloured and were employed in the coastal economy. A whole set of labor regulations were promulgated to control South Africa's first real native proletarians, including the Masters and Servants ordinances of 1841, 1856 and 1873 (preventing strikes and desertion), vagrancy laws and a pass law. In the interior Boer communities and the British Natal, a labor tax was imposed periodically to stimulate help in domestic farming.

With the discovery of diamonds in 1867 at Kimberly and of gold in 1886 at Witwatersrand, the first demands for both white and black labor on a large scale arose.[9] Foreign capital rapidly flowed into the area and the period of primary industrialization began. This activity produced a significant market for agricultural produce, boosting commercial farming and the need for labor in that sector of the economy. In the mining sector, both diamond mines and gold mines formed associations to regulate wages and working conditions in a non-competitive manner and keep labor costs as low as possible.

Except for those in diamond mining, commercial enterprises soon had difficulty recruiting new black labor from within South Africa.[10] On the one hand, a great deal of land was still available for African farming; European commercial farmers faced stiff competition in producing for the domestic market. On the other hand, the mechanisms of proletarianization and forced labor were still not terribly refined or efficiently administered. From 1890 to 1910, the gold mines had to go to Portuguese East Africa and even China to recruit much of their workforce.

The first step toward solving this labor problem was taken during the last 25 years of the 19th century, when whites gained complete political and military hegemony over the area now constituting South Africa.[11] Regions containing independent African communities were brought under control, remaining armed blacks were disarmed, and a tax on indigenous peoples was comprehensively imposed so that everyone would have to participate in the capitalist economy to some extent. At the same time, political and economic conflicts between Boer farming interests and British mining interests came to a head, climaxing in 1899 with the Anglo-Boer War. Out of the British victory came the consolidation of the Cape, Natal, Transvaal and Orange Free State regions (the latter two formerly independent and under the Boers) into the Union of South Africa in 1910.

The development of a strong, central government represented a crucial precondition to the further growth of the economy. Under this new political structure, the conditions for generating an adequate supply of cheap labor were rapidly legislated. In 1911, the Native Labour Regulations Act came into existence, adding mining to those provisions of the earlier Masters and Servants ordinances that made African strikes a crime. With the passage of the Native Land Act in 1913, Africans were allocated 13% of the land in South Africa, and prohibited from purchasing plots outside of this "reserved" area. Thus possibilities for subsistence and/or commercial agriculture on the part of indigenous peoples were severely restricted, increasing the flow of migrant labor to white commercial farms and mines.[12] Of equal importance, whites could not purchase land in the regions reserved for Africans. This provision grew out of a recognition that the cheapness of African labor depended in part on its having some ties to the land. Black workers still received a significant portion of their means of subsistence not through wages but from limited food production in the reserves, so the reserves had to be protected from the encroachment of expanding capitalist agriculture.[13]

In 1918 African workers in both rural and urban areas formed the Industrial and Commercial Workers' Union. Although restricted by law, this and other non-white organizations were developing at a disconcertingly rapid pace.[14] If Africans could effectively organize, especially in the urban areas, the continuance of low wages in the short run and white control of political power in the long run would be challenged. So in 1923 the Native (Urban Areas) Act was legislated. The Urban Areas Act further systematized control over the geographical movements of Africans in South Africa. All adult males had to carry passes, giving their work history and biography; these governed where they could live, work, travel and labor. Individuals could be directed to areas where their labor was needed and away from places where their presence constituted an economic or political threat.

While the growing capitalist economy had been relying on migrant black workers for unskilled positions, skilled and semi-skilled ones were being filled by trained European immigrants and poor white South Africans who had lost their land to commercial agriculture. Even though these individuals occupied the upper tiers of the job structure, their status was ultimately insecure in the face of the extreme cheapness of coerced, non-unionized black labor. When the premium price of gold fell at the close of World War I, mine owners began substituting black labor for the more expensive whites, threatening both the employment and wage level of the latter. Major strikes and unrest on the part of white labor followed, climaxing in a violent insurrection in 1922 (the Rand Revolt). Since unlike Africans these whites possessed the vote, as well as many needed industrial skills, their cooperation with owners of capital in developing the economy

15

was essential.[15]

Consequently, in 1924 the Industrial Conciliation Act became law, setting up a collective bargaining system that only recognized white and coloured trade unions, and in effect limited certain jobs to whites. Practically all African workers were excluded from the legal definition of "employees," preventing them from forming their own legitimate unions or joining recognized ones.[16] This precluded any significant joint action by white and black labor, and institutionalized the privileged status of the white workers. In this manner, the continued support of white labor in exploiting blacks was ensured.

Looking back on the evolution of South African race relations up until the early inter-war years as just described, one sees that the subservient situation of Africans resulted from various laws and institutions. Far from being ends in themselves, i.e., expressions of white race prejudice and cultural chauvinism, such policies were a response to the dynamics of a capitalist economic system attempting to establish itself at the southern tip of the African continent. First this meant attaining political dominance over the indigenous population through acquiring a monopoly on the use of force. Then it meant utilizing such superiority to force the African population out of its pre-capitalist subsistence food production and social arrangements into migratory labor. Finally, it meant insuring that the conditions which kept this labor cheap could be sustained. Although the white workers clearly benefited (and continue to benefit) from this state of affairs, their collaboration has largely been a defensive reaction to the insecurity of being in the same labor market as Africans who could be forced to work at an exceedingly low wage.

All of this is not to say that racial prejudice among whites in South Africa does not exist. On the contrary, racism is rampant and virulent, and strongly influences relations between the races. But these racial attitudes have prospered in South Africa because of their power to give legitimacy to the existing distribution of wealth and power. Racism represents a traditional rationalization for white dominance and black subservience.

The Function of Apartheid

In the years following the period described above, an even more complex system of discrimination and segregation emerged in South Africa. This sytem—commonly known as apartheid—is viewed by progressive force advocates as anachronistic, a holdover from a rural age which has no relevance in a modern, industrial society. C.W. de Kiewiet, a South African historian of the liberal school from which progressive force ideology has in many ways descended, described apartheid in 1956 as "a mental toy, operating outside history and economics."[17] The concept that apartheid has been irrelevant and even dysfunctional to South African economic development constitutes the second crucial assumption implicit in the progressive force argument.

Like the first set of assumptions from which it derives, this notion about the contemporary irrelevance of apartheid is essentially incorrect. Since its inception in the late 1940's, apartheid has been quite forward-looking. Apartheid is a modern mechanism for preserving and regulating the flow of black labor in and out of industry. As the latter portion of the 19th century in South Africa was chiefly occupied with stimulating the labor migration of Africans, the past three decades of the 20th have been primarily occupied with ensuring that such migration does not ultimately undermine white supremacy.

In the late 1920's, those mechanisms of forced labor which had thus far sustained the economy started to become inadequate. This was in large part due to changes in the structure of the economy itself.[18] No longer limited to mining and commercial farming, South Africa began to undergo a period of secondary industrialization. Extreme income inequality produced a great deal of saving by the wealthy which was availble for domestic investment. Depression, war and tariff policies protected infant industries from competition with imports, while government enterprises were formed to channel profits from mining and agriculture into industry. Foreign companies cooperated in providing technology and additional capital.

These developments escalated the demand for African labor. A growing group of heavy industries like electricity and steel required masses of unskilled African workers, at the same time as an adolescent light industry, e.g. textiles, was increasingly in need of semi-skilled ones.[19] As a consequence, rising numbers of blacks were being brought into settings where they could potentially form associations for political and economic advancement. And associate they did. Despite the denial of legal recognition and outright repression, African unions continually formed. Among these was the Council of Non-European Trade Unions, which in 1945 had over 100,000 members.[20] By the mid-1940's at least 40% of African workers in commerce and private industry had been unionized as intermittent subscribers or paid-up members.[21] In 1946, 70,000 black mineworkers went on strike under the banner of the African Mine Workers Union. Such organized activities were symptomatic of the growing presence and entrenchment of Africans in urban areas.[22]

While economic growth provided a pull factor, the role of the reserves as a reservoir and sustainer of black labor was rapidly being undermined, pushing Africans to the cities. Because of loss of male labor through migration, perpetuation of antiquated farming methods, continuous soil erosion and rapid population growth, the African reserves became completely impoverished, only yielding below subsistence crops.[23] As rural Africans sought to escape this environment, they trekked to the cities and set up large shanty towns on their outskirts. Between 1921 and 1945, the urban African population trebled, so that one in four black South Africans were in urban areas by the end of World War II. Moreover, the population was becoming more permanent, with the ratio of African women to men in the cities rising from 1:5 in 1921 to 1:3 in 1945.[24]

From the perspective of white South Africa, this represented an untenable state of affairs. As the South African Board of Trade and Industries stated in 1945:

> The detribalization of large numbers of Natives congregated in amorphous masses in large industrial centres is a matter which no government can view with equanimity. Unless handled with great foresight and skill these masses of detribalized Natives can very easily develop into a menace rather than a constructive factor in industry . . . [25]

A debate ensued over what constituted skillful resolution of the problem. Generally one of two options was advocated, both designed to preserve the status quo.[26]

• A substantial but not complete integration of Africans into urban society. This meant phasing out the migrant system for the more advanced sectors of the economy, giving to those workers permanent residence rights, and in general subsidizing the standard of living required in the city, in areas such as housing and welfare. Black labor would still be kept relatively cheap by outlawing strikes, insuring differential access to education, enforcing limited pass laws, etc.

• Reverse the entrenchment of a growing black urban proletariat, generalizing the system of migrant labor to the newer sectors of the economy through more refined and powerful instruments. This meant halting the breakdown of pre-World War II segregation by implementing: tighter urban influx control, stiffer restrictions on African union activity, strikes and political organizing, increased efficiency in labor recruitment and assignment from the reserves, redevelopment of the reserves to handle some social control and welfare functions, and decentralization of some industry to place it in or near the reserves.

The second option—now referred to as apartheid—was carried forth in the political arena primarily by the Afrikaner-based National Party. The 1947 platform of the Nationalists stated:

> . . . the Bantu in the urban areas should be regarded as migratory citizens not entitled to political or social rights equal to those of the Whites. The process of detribalization should be arrested.[27]

The Nationalists won the 1948 election and have been the ruling white party in South Africa ever since. Their commitment to apartheid has been reaffirmed countless times in the past 30 years.

An ideology of apartheid also emerged, mainly under the direction of Dr. Hendrik Verwoerd, later to be Prime Minister himself. It is important to distinguish between this ideology—known as separate development—and the actual policy of apartheid.[28] The central concept of separate development is that South Africa can never be a multiracial country with integrated citizenship for all races; instead there must be multinational development within the present borders of the country. Because such enormous cultural and social differences between black and white exist, it is argued, there can never be coexistence in a common society. Nonwhites " . . . must be given the opportunity of developing in their own areas and in accordance with their own nature and abilities under guardianship of the Whites . . . "[29] Within this framework Africans are supposed to pursue their social and political lives in the Bantustans, tribal homelands carved out of the 13% of South Africa reserved for blacks.

While the total separation of black and white in South Africa is the logical end of separate development, the ideal has never been seriously pursued as an actual goal of apartheid. Its impossibility was acknowledged by Verwoerd himself in 1948:

> Nobody will deny that for the native as well as for the European complete separation would have been the ideal if it had developed that way histori-cally.[30]

But, he went on to say, this was not "within the realm of possibility."

What has been within the realm of possibility and pursued in practice by apartheid is the actively enforced economic, social, and political dis-enfranchisement of Africans. It is intended to compensate for the increasing reliance on blacks in the labor force, a trend which left uncontrolled would eventually jeopardize white political dominance. With the loss of this political dominance, the handle on those instruments of coercion guaranteeing cheap labor would also be forfeited.[31]

The system of apartheid as it has developed over the past 30 years has consisted of five major policies. Each of these policies has been implemented through specific laws and administrative practices, a description of which reflects how apartheid conforms to the political and economic exigencies of post-World War II South Africa.

Influx Control

Influx control insures that only those Africans essential to the operation of the economy will be present in urban areas.[32] Those living in the reserves who would go to the cities and take their chances, if migration were unrestricted, are bottled up in their "homelands." Migrant workers who might otherwise bring their families to the urban areas are forced to leave behind such "surplus appendages" as wives, children, and parents. And when African labor is in surplus, as in periods of economic recession, unemployed workers can be sent away from the virtual doorsteps of their employers and into the barren wastelands of the country.

This is achieved through the Bantu (Urban Areas) Act of 1945, as amended and by the Bantu Laws Amendment Act of 1964. Under these laws, no African can be in an urban area without certain special qualifications or a job; no African can enter an urban area without previously obtaining an employment contract through a government labor bureau; no African can continue to reside in an urban area without periodically reapplying for permission to stay. Blacks in the urban areas for whatever reasons are subject to being "endorsed out" to the reserves by an administrative order.

Labor Recruitment and Restrictions on Unionization

While white South Africa has worked to keep unneeded Africans out of the urban areas, it has also developed a system to control those individuals whose labor it does require. This involves the capacity to channel labor where it is needed and to keep it from exerting pressure for wage increases via unionization once it is there.

To direct black labor geographically, a national system of labor bureaus has been established.[33] All unemployed African males must report to the bureaus, and with a few exceptions, employers can only hire workers who have registered. An African who does not report can be arrested without warrant and removed from his area. A bureau can cancel an existing contract, and it can bar an African worker from being in the employment of anyone. For blacks who refuse employment, the "idle" or "undesirable" classification can be assigned; those who receive it can be sent to a work colony for up to three years.

To impede any efforts of Africans to organize trade unions aimed at improving their material status, a series of acts have been legislated: the Industrial Conciliation Act of 1924 (discussed previously), the Industrial Conciliation Act of 1956, the Bantu Labor (Settlement of Disputes) Act of 1953, and the Bantu Labor Regulation Act of 1964.[34]

African trade unions cannot receive legal recognition nor the legal rights accompanying such recognition. By law they cannot be registered and are consequently excluded from the industrial council and collective bargaining system. Nor can Africans join registered white or coloured unions. Strikes by black workers are illegal (except in very restricted situations). Those participating may be fined $1400 and jailed for up to 3 years. Or perhaps more likely, they will find themselves endorsed out to the reserves. Finally, African workers are held in tight rein by making breaches of contract criminal offenses.

Colour Bar

As noted above, barring blacks from certain types of work has generally been a concession to the white workers' concern over competition with artificially cheap African labor. It is mainly implemented through stipulations in contracts negotiated by white unions and employers at an industry-wide level. In addition, blacks are by both custom and law denied access to certain kinds of vocational and artisan training. While efforts toward establishing a colour bar in the pre-apartheid years were fairly piecemeal, a more general colour bar was erected by the Industrial Conciliation Act of 1956.[35] It empowers the Minister of Labor to investigate any economic enterprise and then: prohibit the replacement of workers of one race by workers of another race; reserve a class of work or jobs for members of a specified race; compel employers to maintain a fixed percentage of workers of a particular race; fix maximum, minimum or average numbers or percentages of persons of a particular race who may be employed in any place of work. The Minister of Labour may grant exemptions to the colour bar, allowing a crucial flexibility in its application.

Pass Laws

All of these policies are administered with the assistance of a population registration apparatus commonly known as the Pass Laws.[36] Under the Bantu (Abolition of Passes and Co-ordination of Documents) Act of 1952, all Africans over 16 must carry an identity document called a Reference Book. It contains the identity number and photograph of the bearer, his ethnic group, nation or tribe, the name and address of his employer, date of his engagement, and details of taxes, levies and rates paid by him. Each month the book must be signed by his employer and a date of discharge noted when work is terminated. For African women the book must include the name, address and reference book number of her husband, parent or guardian. These books must be produced on demand. In 1975 alone approximately 400,000 people were prosecuted under pass laws, and hundreds of thousands more were stopped.[37]

At the end of 1977 the government disclosed a plan to replace passbooks with travel documents to be issued by the Bantustans. Travel document holders, however, will be subject to the same kind of laws, requirements, and restrictions that have plagued black South Africans under the passbook system. "The document is different. The disabilities are the same," commented the president of Black Sash, an organization

21

that tries to help people prosecuted for pass law violations.[38]

The Bantustans

It is the Bantustan system which supplies the labor that is regulated by influx control, recruitment bureaus, and the colour bar. All Africans are assigned a Bantustan homeland which is their legal residence. They live and work in the white areas only at the pleasure of their employers (Bantu Homeland Citizenship Act—1970).[39] The Bantustans are an integral part of the South African economic system—they represent South Africa's "reserve army of unemployed" and are a key component of the South African migratory labor system.

While the idea of establishing "native reserves" for the Africans is almost as old as the European occupation of South Africa, the present Bantustan system basically has been constructed since 1951. The same legislation that set up the Bantustans also terminated most of the civil rights held by Africans. Starting with the Bantu Authorities Act, No. 68 of 1951 and continuing with such legislation as the Promotion of Bantu Self-Government Act, No. 46 of 1959, the Promotion of the Economic Development of Bantu Homelands Act, No. 26 of 1970 and so on—right up to the present—the National Party has tried to shape a Bantustan policy that can both serve the reality of South Africa's need for cheap African labor, and the illusion of African self-government.[40]

The first of these goals has been met; the second has not. The Bantustans are economically unviable, and most are not even geographically whole. They are scattered in 81 separate and non-contiguous pieces of land. Although theoretically the home of all Africans, the nine Bantustans make up only 13% of the land area. Neither of the two nominally independent Bantustans, the Transkei and Bophuthatswana, has been recognized by any country other than South Africa. All the Bantustans are policed by the South African military and security apparatus. The Bantu Homelands Constitution Act, No. 21 of 1971, prohibits Bantustan legislatures from dealing with matters of defense, foreign affairs, immigration, banking, customs and excise, railways, harbors, national roads, civil aviation, postal, telegraph, telephone and radio services. [41]

While the South African government hasn't successfully made the migratory labor pattern apply to 100% of the work force, it remains committed to an expansion of the Bantustan system. The desire of the Nationalists to extend the 'homelands' citizenship is stated unambiguously by M.C. Botha, former Minister of Bantu Administration and Development. "As far as I'm concerned the ideal condition would be if we could succeed in due course in having all Bantu present in the white areas on a basis of migratory labour only."[42] Yet South Africa needs the labor of the black majority—"for the sake of the white economy," as Mr.

Froneman, Deputy Minister for Justice put it. "Without them it would be impossible to maintain the essential growth rate . . . "[43]

The ideology of apartheid was hammered out to reconcile the threat posed by urban blacks and the need for their labor. As Prime Minister John Vorster said in 1968:

"It is true that there are blacks working for us. They will continue to work for us for generations, in spite of the ideal we have to separate them completely.
. . . The fact of the matter is this: we need them, because they work for us . . . but the fact that they work for us can never entitle them to claim political rights. Not now, nor in the future.[44]

Commitment to this policy remains constant; it is the terminology that changes. "Plural democracy" is used in place of separate development, and the Department of Bantu Administration and Development (BAD) is now called Plural Relations and Development. In fact, a 1978 General Law Amendment Act calls for dropping the term Bantu altogether.

The Coercive Apparatus

The element of the apartheid system which makes it possible for a small minority to dominate the majority of the population is the violent power of the South African state and its coercive apparatus. A dense network of repressive legislation gives the security forces a wide range of options in dealing with all kinds of dissent.

There are 59 separate laws, passed since the Nationalists came to power, that are designed to protect the security of the state. The Suppression of Communism Act, No. 44 of 1950 gives the Minister of Justice broad powers to restrict persons suspected of promoting communism. Communism is so loosely defined that it includes any action which might oppose the government through promoting disturbances, unlawful activities, or hostilities between white and black.

This act sets up the punishment of banning which means the banned person cannot hold public office, belong to specified organizations, attend meetings, leave defined areas, or speak to the media. In many cases those banned cannot meet with more than one person at a time.[45]

Under the Riotous Assemblies Act, the Justice Minister may prohibit any gathering. The Public Safety Act, No. 3 of 1953 allows for the declaration of a state of emergency at any time and gives the police unrestricted power in such cases. Section 6 of the Terrorism Act, No. 83 of 1967 empowers the police to arrest any person believed to be a terrorist or to be withholding information about terrorists. Terrorism is broadly defined as intent to endanger the maintenance of law and order. Such a person may be detained anywhere in South Africa for any length of time.

23

Detainees are held in solitary confinement without being allowed to see their family or lawyers, nor is the family even told of the detainee's whereabouts.[46]

Along with the consistent use of this repressive legislation, the south African security forces have often resorted to the use of terror and the murder of detained subjects.[47] The brutality and repressive nature of the white South African regime is condemned by many supporters of the progressive force argument. What must be faced is that this brutality and repression is a key part of the apartheid system, a system that will go a long way to defend—and perpetuate—itself.

Taken as a whole, apartheid legislation has successfully perpetuated the conditions which guarantee a cheap black labor force. Although black workers in South Africa do not routinely labor under the whip of a white task master, their labor is nonetheless forced. This was noted by a United Nations' committee from the International Labor Organization which investigated African labor in South Africa in 1953. In regard to the system of apartheid the committee concluded:

> The ultimate consequence of the system is to compel the native population to contribute, by their labour, to the implementation of the economic policies of the country, but the compulsory and involuntary nature of this contribution results from the peculiar status and situation created by special legislation applicable to the indigenous inhabitants alone, rather than from direct coercive measures designed to compel them to work, although such measures, which are the inevitable consequence of this status, were also found to exist.
>
> It is in this indirect sense therefore that, in the Committee's view, a system of forced labor of significance to the national economy appears to exist in the Union of South Africa.[48]

Since the U.N. report much of the more onerous legislation has been implemented by the South African government.

The effectiveness of apartheid can be seen in the exceptional performance of the South African economy in the two decades following the 1948 Nationalist triumph. Between 1950 and 1972, the Gross Domestic Product (at constant 1963 prices) increased from $3.7 billion to $13.9 billion.[49] National income doubled between 1946 and 1960, and the next decade saw even more phenomenal expansion.[50] The 1960's was a period of extraordinary growth—about 6% annual real growth for the economy as a whole and 7% in manufacturing.[51] Only Japan and Germany surpassed this figure. South Africa now accounts for two-thirds of the African continent's steel production and 40% of all electricity generated.[52]

Post-apartheid boom has produced substantial profits for private investors and a very high standard of living for white South Africa. Return on investment has been well above world levels. For example, American subsidiaries in South Africa earned an average rate of return of 18.6% between 1960 and 1970, while U.S. direct investments worldwide had a considerably lower 11% average rate of return.[53] While per capita personal income as of 1974/75 amounted to R2534 (about $3000), placing South African whites near the top of the world income rankings.[54]

It is clear that this economic vigor has in large part resulted from South Africa's cheap black labor policy. At a September 1975 meeting of the Economic Society of South Africa, J. Nattrass of Natal University reported that her research on migrant black labor had led to the conclusion that the white economy has substantially benefited from the apartheid system in three ways. First, workers, directed to their places of work under the system, have had no bargaining strength, keeping profits and white wages high and investment buoyant. Moreover, employers have paid less believing that black workers' families need not be supported because they are in the homelands. Finally, the economy has not had to divert resources from directly productive investment into housing workers and their families in urban areas.[55]

Far from being irrelevant or dysfunctional to the rise of modern, industrial South Africa, apartheid has been the basis of such development. At a time when change threatened the continuance of white rule in the 1940's, the National Party responded with a pragmatic policy to preserve dominant political and economic interests. This policy has meant enormous material progress for white South Africa, a fact which directly contradicts the progressive force position that there is a fundamental conflict between economic growth in South Africa and discriminatory measures against blacks. The idea that continued development of the economy is incompatible with maintaining apartheid represents the third and most crucial assumption of the progressive force position.

The Compatibility of Apartheid and Economic Growth

Progressive force advocates argue that industrial growth continually intensifies the need for skilled labor in South Africa, yet the white population is becoming insufficient as a source of such workers.[56] This means that more blacks must be trained for and employed in jobs formerly held by whites. But, it is claimed, promotion of blacks to these positions cannot be accomplished without significantly weakening apartheid. Africans will have to be paid more and migrate less. Ultimately, they argue, this will produce an entrenched, unionized black workforce which will have the power to demand those things which it has for so long been denied. The alternative to this scenario is economic stagnation. In regard to this point Harry Oppenheimer has argued, "A country that refuses to allow something like 80% of its labor force to do the best work of which they are capable cannot hope to progress as it should or hold its place in a highly competitive world."[57]

It is this skilled labor problem that explains why U.S. firms operating in South Africa are said to be promoting equal opportunity. According to the Investor Responsibility Research Center, "The greatest pressure companies mention is economic: they need a larger pool of workers to draw from." The IRRC goes on to state:

> In the last few years, the economic pressures on [U.S.] corporations to adopt progressive labor practices have increased significantly. Shortages of skilled workers, inflated wages demanded by whites, and high turnover, high absenteeism and low productivity for white workers, all have offered sound economic reasons for a manager in South Africa to make efforts to recruit and train blacks and place them in positions which have traditionally been held by whites in order to achieve a more stable and productive work force.[58]

By working aggressively to meet this challenge, United States companies are supposed to make a major contribution to the welfare of the non-white population.

The gap between the amount of skilled labor needed for growth and the available pool of trained workers under current conditions is real. Depending on the study one quotes, this gap is growing by several thousand jobs annually. Businessmen have strongly criticized the job colour bar, desiring a freer hand in substituting black labor for white. Yet available evidence suggests that the skilled labor needs of the economy can be met without making fundamental changes in apartheid. And there is evidence that whatever upgrading of African job status does take place in the foreseeable future will not ultimately shatter the cornerstones of white domination.

First of all, future changes in the nature of the black workforce must be put in perspective. The economic integration of blacks and whites in South Africa has been proceeding rapidly for several decades with little positive impact on the overall status of Africans in the country. Millions of blacks have been shifted out of subsistence agriculture into wage employment. In 1946 there were 2.9 million economically active blacks; this figure had increased by 140% to 6.9 million in 1975. Over 70% of the entire South African labor force is black.[59] Nor are these African workers just out in the mines or commercial agricultural fields. More than one in ten work in manufacturing, with the absolute number in this sector (756,000) having increased 200% over 1950 levels. The 256,000 black manufacturing workers who hold semi-skilled operative positions account for the majority of all employees in this sector's operative job category.[60]

In comparison to the massive shift of millions of blacks into the manufacturing sector, the current effort to fill the white labor gap cannot be expected to mean more than the promotion of a few thousand black workers each year. Following a major manpower survey in 1974, the Minister of Labour reported that to maintain a planned 6.4% rate of growth through 1979 "5,000 black workers a year would have to be drawn into positions left vacant by the white labour shortage."[61] Data from the Human Sciences Research Council quoted by Van der Merwe suggests that this figure might be a little higher, perhaps 6,000 or 7,000.[62] While such upgradings would over time represent significant increases in the absolute number of black skilled workers in the labor force, they would be quite marginal in terms of the job status distribution of the black work force as a whole. For example, promoting 6,000 individuals out of the current black employee pool will mean shifting less than one out of 1000 African workers into a projected white vacancy—at a time when it is estimated that more than 100,000 new black employees enter the labor force annually.[63] According to the Information Counselor of the South African Embassy in Washington, D.C., "Each year more than 250,000 new workers pour into the job market."[64]

One must also consider the process employed thus far to put African workers in jobs formerly reserved for whites. The controlled promotion of blacks into semi-skilled and skilled jobs has been going on for several years. Replacing a white worker with a black has typically meant denying to the new employee the same status and pay of the old. According to the 1973 report from SPROCAS, a group of liberal white South African academics:

> Legal job reservation restrictions in practice now apply to very few jobs, except in the building and mining industries. Conditions are often incorporated into the exemption orders [issued by the Minister of Labor] which allow lower wage rates for black workers, or the denial of the status and rights which should attach to the job. Where the exemption is granted for blacks to do work usually reserved for whites it is often accompanied by the rationalization that this is only a 'temporary' measure so that, although the temporary nature of the measure is never subjected to proof, black workers have no real security of job tenure.[65]

Employers can continue to take advantage of the relatively weak bargaining position of the upgraded African employees, while they must persist in pacifying their white labor force in a manner preserving the latter's superiority and job security. Frequently special bonus pay hikes are given to white unions to gain their support for relaxing the colour bar.

The actual techniques used to place Africans in white positions illustrate how flexible the apartheid system can be while still retaining its discriminatory features.[66] Some jobs are renamed before being allotted to black workers; for example, the creation of "building assistants" in construction or "artisan assistants" on the railways. These newly labelled slots are given wage rates considerably less than those prevailing under their former names.

Even more common is the method known as job fragmentation or job dilution. Skilled work formerly done by one white employee is broken down into two or more less skilled tasks. Lower paid and less trained blacks are then brought in to do the new jobs—with their total wage bill amounting to less than what one white was being paid. Africans in manufacturing on average make 4 to 5 times less than whites in this sector. E.H. McCann, General Secretary of the (white) South African Amalgamated Engineering Union, described job fragmentation in the following manner:

> This is a process whereby one part of a skilled artisan's work is given to a less skilled individual who as a result can be paid slightly more than he was receiving as a pure laborer. In this way we have helped to create a large force of semi-skilled workers whose pay is substantially less than that of skilled workers.[67]

These facts go a long way in explaining how the absolute gap between white and black income continues to widen even as African workers are shifted into jobs they never held before. In 1970, the average white household had R362 more to spend each month than the average African household. By 1975, the gap had widened to R546.[68]

Progressive force advocates contend that one feature of apartheid doomed to extinction with the upgrading of the black labor force's skill level is the migratory labor system. A labor force which annually oscillates between the Bantustans and places of work has a notoriously high rate of turnover. It will be inefficient and too costly to invest in expensive training for workers who may not be back next year. Increasingly black workers must remain in the same firm to acquire necessary skills, meaning that migratory labor will be phased out.

In reality the government has developed and will continue to introduce innovative labor controls which significantly stabilize the black workforce *without* ending its migratory character. One such recent invention is the call-in card system.[69] The call-in card system guarantees that an African worker who wants to be reassigned to the same employer will be so directed after his annual trek back to the Bantustan. Ordinarily a worker might be channeled into any number of jobs with a variety of employers when his labor contract is renewed yearly at the appropriate Bantu labor bureau. But by being issued a call-in card from his employer, the black laborer can be automatically reassigned to his old position. Accordingly, employers can be assured that their investment in skilled African workers will not be lost through the vagaries and complications of the migrant system. Yet the African worker remains a migrant, legally rooted in the homelands with family and possessions, having nearly the same status as a less skilled position. In 1975, approximately 255,000 blacks were handled through the call-in card system, and the number appears to be increasing rapidly.[70]

The call-in card system came to prominence with modifications in the labor control bureaucracy during the early 1970's. These included the formation of 22 Bantu Affairs Administration Boards and increased utilization of computers in managing the labor supply. These Boards assumed control of labor bureaus from local authorities. Prior to this change a black worker could only be employed in an urban area for which he had residential qualifications or local authorization. Now an African worker can take up employment within the much larger jurisdiction of the Administration Board.[71] The government has stated that

> . . . employers benefit from this enhanced mobility because it ensures not only a more ready availability of labour as such but also of labour suited to their specific needs. Every labour bureau endeavors to meet the demand for labour from sources within its own area of jurisdiction; migratory labour from areas controlled by other bureaus is introduced on a supplementary basis only—to meet specific shortages which may occur.[72]

Among other uses, this new structure has allowed the placement of "urban insider" blacks in jobs which require a high degree of employment stability. Giving relatively entrenched Africans, those born or of long residence in white areas, differential access to such skilled positions further guarantees that influx control and the migrant system will not have to be phased out in order to meet the economy's labor requirements.[73]

Indeed, rather than decreasing in importance, the migrant labor system has become more prominent as a method for bringing Africans into the urban industrial sector. This is in direct contradiction to what the progressive force argument would lead one to expect. It is crucial because migrancy significantly weakens the bargaining strength of black workers. Francis Wilson, a faculty member at the University of Cape Town, is the foremost student of migrant labor in South Africa. In a 1975 paper he reports that there has been a

> . . . rapid expension since the mid-1960's of a migrant labor system in the manufacturing sector similar to that which has existed for three generations in the gold mines . . . in industrial areas where there are no mine compounds the proportion of migrants is very substantial and seems to have increased markedly in recent years.[74]

Wilson notes that in cities such as Cape Town, 85% of all black men are living in migrant housing (compounds and hostels). Research by Nattrass supports these conclusions.[75] In regard to the migrant system she states that "the situation has grown steadily worse as South Africa has developed. Continuing development has meant a continued growth in the size of the stream of temporary migrants." She estimates that since 1936 the number of migrants has grown at a compound rate of 3.1% a year. Since World War II the number has grown faster than the number of Africans in employment. By 1970 approximately 59% of all African men working in white areas were migrants. And if we include blacks who live year-round in the homelands and travel daily to work in white areas, then this figure is between 80% and 90%.

Industrial Relations and the Black Labor Movement

The crucial bridge between the advancing position of blacks in the workplace and greater economic and political power for Africans, according to progressive force advocates, is the formation of African trade unions. They argue that as blacks become increasingly critical to industrial operations the need for good capital-labor communication will increase, with the implicit bargaining power of blacks increasingly institutionalized in recognized trade unions. Like previous progressive force claims about the social and political impact of economic growth, this point is open to challenge on several grounds.

The black labor movement in South Africa has a long history, but effective rights to organize, bargain, and strike remain a fantasy under the laws of apartheid. The Industrial and Commercial Workers' Union (ICU) had at least 200,000 members at the height of its power in 1928,[76] and as noted earlier, its successor, the Council of Non-European Trade Unions (CNETU) claimed 119 affiliates and a combined membership of 158,000 by 1945.[77] Without exception, however, the surges in growth and power of the movement have been followed by massive suppression.

When the Nationalist government introduced the Bantu Labour (Settlement of Disputes) Act in 1953, loopholes in the definition of "employee" were closed, absolutely excluding all Africans from registered trade unions and collective bargaining. Moreover, all strikes were prohibited.[78] "Works committees" at each plant were to handle negotiation and settlement of disputes, but employers were not required to negotiate with them. The Minister of Labour at the time, Mr. Schoeman, told Parliament that since the government could not prevent African unions from "being used as a political weapon," it intended to "bleed them to death."[79]

Nevertheless, new life was added to the labor movement when the South African Congress of Trade Unions (SACTU) was formed in 1955. SACTU became a member of the Congress Alliance, made up of the African National Congress, the S.A. Indian Congress, the S.A. Coloured People's Organization, and the Congress of Democrats. By 1961, SACTU had 46 affiliated unions and had succeeded in organizing thousands of new workers.[80]

Then repression once more hit hard at all mass organizations. Raids, bannings, and arrests forced SACTU to go underground in 1967. Official harassment had also forced another smaller federation, an ICFTU affiliate with ties to the Pan Africanist Congress, to disband in 1966.[81]

Victimization of union leadership, intimidation by employers and the government, and police repression have continued to curtail black unionization. Despite expansion of the African labor force, black union membership in the late 70's is probably no larger than in the early 1960's. (In 1975, black unregistered trade unions were estimated to have 50,000 to 75,000 members organized into approximately 25 separate groups.)[82]

There was, however, another resurgence of energy in the black trade union movement following a series of strikes in Natal in 1973. 361 strikes and work stoppages, involving over 90,000 Africans took place in 1973, and the first half of 1974 saw 54 more strikes. In virtually all the disputes, the police were called in, and nearly 1000 African workers were arrested.[83]

In response to this unrest the government passed the Bantu Labour Relations Regulation Act of 1973. The new act supplemented works committees with "liaison committees." The effectiveness of the former in meeting workers' demands can be judged from the fact that 20 years after they were established, there were only 24 works committees in a country with some 21,036 factories.[84] In a liaison committee only half the members are chosen by black workers; management selects the chairperson and the other half. Only if an employer has not chosen to establish a liaison committee first, can a works committee now be set up. It is no wonder that employer-dominated liaison committees, consultative bodies only, are preferred by management and, hence, are far more numerous. By April 1976, 290 works committees and 2,167 liaison committees had been formed, the overwhelming majority (91% in one study) at the employer's initiative.[85]

The committee system is part of an ongoing effort to open a "channel of communication" between labor and management within individual plants so the latter will be able to neutralize potential disruption. According to the Deputy Director of the AFL-CIO's African American Labor Center, the system is "an attempt to set up machinery for settling black labor troubles without allowing black workers to really organize into effective trade unions."[86]

Another method, adopted by the Trade Union Council of South Africa (TUCSA), has been the establishment of parallel unions for Africans. In the case of one white registered union, the motive was clear—"to protect our members' living standards in the face of a growing flood of Africans into the industry." To maintain its power, TUCSA has had to control the organizing of black workers, keep registered unions dominant and white wages higher, and prevent black unions from getting involved in political actions. TUCSA's position with regard to the affiliation of black unions has shifted so often that their intentions are suspect to many black workers, especially since the record shows that the registered unions often manipulate and sometimes actually run the parallel unions.[87]

So African workers are still not allowed to directly represent themselves, and their wages are set for them by (1) registered unions and employers, (2) the State, or (3) a group of employers alone. Moreover, the strategy for dealing with African labor organizing continues to be outright repression or removal. Government-orchestrated brutality disrupted the three-day general strike called after the Soweto riots of June 1976. The police armed, transported, and urged Soweto hostel dwellers to kill strikers. Besides the fatalities from street fighting, union organizers were banned and arrested, and three later died in detention.[88] In June 1977, 800 African miners who were on strike were fired and shipped back to the Bantustans the next day.[89] When the entire work force of 600 at Heinemann Electric Company, partly American-owned, it was dismissed because it wanted representation through trade unions instead of committees, eyewitnesses reported that after a meeting,

> 27 policemen wielding batons charged the workers from behind. There was panic and confusion . . . several people were bitten by police dogs. Some 14 people were taken to the hospital . . . Five people were arrested under the Riotous Assemblies Act and the Police Act.[90]

While iron-fist tactics, growing unemployment, and preemption of some disputes through the committee system have diminished the incidence of strikes, labor unrest has not been eradicated. The current policies of both government and industry are under review, but what has transpired since 1973 indicates how the problem may be "resolved" in the future. It suggests the limited impact that government recognition of black trade unions would have.

First of all, any government recognition of black rights to collectively bargain and strike will be a double-edged sword for African workers. On the one hand, it will protect the unions from much of the harassment they now suffer and force employers to sit down and negotiate. On the other hand, recognition will give the government another source of leverage, for the unions will be subject to new regulation accompanying unionization. It can be expected that the government will exercise this control. First, it might require that all union organizers and bureaucrats be government trained, or be partially under the restraining influence of white unions. Provisions of the Bantu Labour Act of 1973 foreshadow this sort of approach. Although the Act gives the African right-to-strike nominal recognition, it is rendered impotent by the procedures which workers must go through to gain strike authorization.[91]

Secondly, any trade union movement which emerges from the current struggle can be expected to be a fragmented one, subject to the apartheid strategy of divide and rule. There is evidence that when black trade unions are given some sort of real recognition, it will be as "enterprise unions."[92] They will not be national or industry-wide associations, but company or plant-level unions. This trend is reinforced by the organizing tactics which the politics of apartheid force upon the trade union movement—building unions through fairly small, dispersed organizations rather than previous nationwide alliances like CNETU or SACTU. Unions within such a decentralized structure may have a difficult time providing each other with mutual aid.

Thirdly, the organizing domain of African unions will be limited, both by existing legislation outlawing black political activity and future legislation dealing specifically with unions. The major government objection to black unions has been, as Minister of Labor Botha said, that "they could lend themselves to being used as political instruments."[93] It can be expected that much of the state's repressive resources will be focused on keeping African labor activity within bounds that do not threaten the basic status quo. Some black trade union organizers sensitive to this have already been explicitly stating that their concerns will be economic issues, not social and political ones. For example, the General Secretary of the African Transport and Allied Worker's Union has stated:

> We are not for disrupting anything, just for improving the labor situation. We do not concern ourselves with politics, but only with bread and butter issues. We leave politics to the politicians. Trade unions to be successful must keep out of politics.[94]

Fourthly, the history of trade unionism in other underdeveloped labor forces suggests that workers who eventually belong to recognized labor organizations in South Africa might develop rather parochial interests and goals.[95] The success of trade unionism in any context requires exercising some control over labor supply, limiting whom the employer can hire and at what wage. In an economy like South Africa's, where the number of skilled positions will be, for the foreseeable future, quite small relative to the mass of black workers seeking jobs, this exclusiveness will be particularly important. It is very possible that unionized black workers in South Africa will form a "labor aristocracy," moderating the demands they might make on the system. This is what a prominent member of the South African Association of Chambers of Commerce, J.J. Conradie, had in mind last year when he suggested creating a stable middle class of urban black skilled workers and entrepreneurs:

> It is both unsound and dangerous for blacks to be moulded in a single strata of their own without a real middle class.[96]

The same sentiment was echoed by hardline Minister of Justice Jimmy Kruger who in June 1977 said,

> South Africa must create a Black middle class to counter the threat of Black Power . . . [97]

Contrary to the progressive force argument, African trade unions do not appear to represent a very promising avenue of basic social change in South Africa. The migrant labor system and the predominantly unskilled character of the black labor force will persist for at least decades to come. The minority of skilled and upper level semi-skilled workers in the economy do have a real potential for gaining trade union rights, but their power will be limited. South Africa's white government will continue to ultimately define the legitimate activity of black trade unions and suppress trends which represent direct political challenges to apartheid. At best these recognized black unions may raise the wages and job security of a small segment of black South African labor. At worst they may serve as a significant drag on the aspirations of the non-unionized majority of black workers.

For decades coloured (mixed race) workers in South Africa have played a role in the labor force which blacks are only now said to be attaining. Coloureds are guaranteed trade union rights under the Industrial Conciliation Act and serve in leadership positions in the Trade Union Council of South Africa. Yet they are still economically impoverished relative to whites, and their political and social status has markedly deteriorated. Up until 1956 coloureds in Cape Province were listed on the common voting rolls with whites. In that year the government placed them on a separate roll, with power to elect four members to the National Assembly and one to the Senate, provided that the representatives were white.[98] Then in 1968 a completely separate and powerless representative council was set up for coloured affairs, and they lost all rights to vote in the white national political system.[99] Under the Group Areas Act, thousands of coloured families have been forcibly removed from urban areas, where their ancestors had lived for centuries, and relocated in new, segregated townships.[100]

Far from necessitating or producing the breakdown of apartheid, further economic growth is compatible with its basic rationale—optimizing growth within a socioeconomic order that maintains white privilege and power. As Labour Minister Marais Viljoen stated in August 1975:

> . . . the government does not stand in the way of changes in the traditional work patterns which allow non-whites to move up into job categories for which they will require higher skills and in which they can earn higher wages,

provided that changes come about in an orderly fashion and with the con-
currence of [white] trade unions and provided such changes do not result in
the undermining of our social structure and character . . . The more productive utilization of non-white labour in a controlled and orderly manner
is therefore the government's earnest desire.[101]

The point is to make the golden goose as productive as possible, not kill it
in the process.

The attitude of South African business leaders toward apartheid is
quite revealing, for they are sensitive to any economic inefficiencies in the
system. They have been prominent advocates of the progressive force
thesis, and relative to the government, business leaders are said to be
change oriented. In December 1977, ten South African business
organizations stated that they had chosen to "strive constantly for the
elimination of discrimination based on race or colour from all aspects of
employment practice."[102] In the past, such organizations have called for
more liberal treatment of urban blacks and some kind of bargaining rights
for black employees.

There is of course a strong element of public relations hypocrisy in
these Chamber of Commerce pronouncements. For example, no law
stands in the way of businesses going beyond rhetoric and unilaterally
dealing with black trade unions, yet only a handful have done so. Calls for
reforms have been overshadowed by favorable business attitudes toward
apartheid, not unlike those of the National Party itself. In 1971
sociologist Heribert Adams published a survey on racial attitudes of
government and business in South Africa. In interviews with a sample of
English and Afrikaner businessmen, Adam determined two things. On the
one hand, these entrepreneurs were quite critical of government
restrictions on the free use of black labor. On the other hand, Adam found
that

Potential profit restrictions as a consequence of this policy are out-weighed
[for business people] by considerations of internal stability and unlimited
access to abundant cheap labor which still guarantees a comparatively high
return from investment.[103]

These "considerations of internal stability" in part reflect business worries
that a majority-ruled South Africa might be a less hospitable place for
private capital than a white-ruled one. The editor of the *Financial Mail*
wrote in 1976, "The greatest fear I find (among South African
businessmen) is that so little has been done to foster an appreciation of the
values of private enterprise among black people." He reported a growing
concern that as blacks acquire power, "it will fall into the hands of people
who have little sympathy for private enterprise but lead instead to some
form of socialism."[104] Such fear is quite rational; Steve Biko, described as a
potential black prime minister before his death, once said "any black

government is likely to be socialist."[105]

Industry and finance's vision of a future South Africa is incorporated in the program of the Progressive (Federal) Party, their main political vehicle. The Progressives advocate a system which would not enfranchise the vast majority of blacks but only a relative few with high incomes and good education. The Party argues that "only such a program will prolong white rule, by easing the frustrations of the black majority, which will otherwise inevitably explode, bringing down white rule."[106] Thus the only substantial difference between "enlightened" business and the "reactionary" government is over what approach will best preserve black powerlessness.

The progressive force argument claims that achieving healthy economic growth in South Africa is incompatible with maintaining the apartheid system. While it is impossible to demonstrate absolutely that the progressive force scenario will not come about, ample evidence supports the contention that there is nothing inevitable about apartheid being undermined by the process of continued economic growth. On the contrary, it seems more probable that white domination will adapt to economic imperatives while retaining the key features of apartheid. Progressive force advocates tend to exaggerate the demands of economic change and underestimate the durability of repressive institutions.

While future growth will intensify the need for skilled labor and require placing some blacks in positions formerly reserved for whites, the unskilled/semi-skilled character of the African workforce will not be altered substantially. Those blacks who are upgraded in skill level will be denied the status associated with such positions in the past. The call-in card system, changes in the labor control bureaucracy, and other adjustments will enable a segment of the black work force to be stabilized (as a prerequisite for investment in their training) without ending the migrant system. Black trade unions will be accorded increased recognition, but their operation will be fragmented, circumscribed by the larger structure of apartheid, and will have the potential for producing a moderate, labor aristocracy. Finally, as evidenced by the coloured population's experience, the link between economic advancement and socio-political freedom is a tenuous one.

United States corporations operating in South Africa have argued that their labor practices can bring meaningful change to the thousands of non-whites they employ (They employ about 1% of the total African labor force, or approximately 70,000 workers). But the positive role of these companies is fundamentally predicated upon the existence of internal economic forces in South Africa pushing for evolutionary liberalization. If economy-wide changes in employment practices demanded by growth are not sufficient to seriously challenge apartheid, then it is doubtful reforms by foreign firms can do so. Groups within the

U.S. may continue to push for labor reform on the part of American multinationals, but even if successful the changes produced will not undermine white rule.

Even though the potential of progressive action by U.S. firms has limits, it does not mean they have come close to testing them. On the contrary, American companies have not been outstanding in their labor practices. A *Wall Street Journal* article in March 1977 evaluating the equal opportunity performance of U.S. subsidiaries in South Africa cites "a pattern of uneven efforts and sporadic accomplishments in ending job bias."[107] The most extensive study to date of these employment practices, by Desaix Myers of the Investor Responsibility Research Center, states that:

> the bulk of American companies doing business in South Africa probably are no more innovative than South African or British or other foreign business.[108]

Almost 100 American companies have not pledged to work for reform in South Africa by following a set of fair employment principles developed of Reverend Leon Sullivan, a member of the General Motors board. Besides being voluntary and rather vague, the pledge states that modification of working conditions will go through "appropriate channels." Since the Sullivan Principles show little promise for substantive improvement, it is not surprising that the South African government approved them. The *Financial Mail* has called the pledge a "damp squib" (a firecracker that fizzles).[109] Such a term befits not only the efforts of American firms to improve the lives of black South Africans, but the whole progressive force position in general.

II.
The Economic and Political Impact of American Investment in South Africa

Economic growth and foreign investment pose no threat to the system of apartheid. In fact, available evidence shows that U.S. investment in South Africa actually bolsters that system. Even if the employment practices of American firms were judged to be progressive, marginally or otherwise, this positive impact could easily be outweighed by their contributions to the maintenance of apartheid. The past and present pattern of U.S. business involvement in South Africa reveals an ultimatley collaborative relationship with the ruling whites. American investment has concretely assisted in the suppression of African rights, shielding the very target of its supposed progressive employment practices.

The Modernization of Terror

To document the ways in which American investment in South Africa is an accomplice to apartheid, one must begin with a very basic question. How do a little over four million whites in that country control the day to day existence of nearly 22 million non-whites? The answer is coercion, coercion ultimately based on the ability of the government to subject the non-white population to direct violence and terror. Albie Sachs, formerly an attorney in South Africa and Lecturer in Law, University of Southampton, has expressed this point quite clearly:

> ... the ruling class in South Africa has constituted itself into a visibly distinct section of the population and has deliberately eschewed such modes of legitimizing its rule as universalizing franchise rights or education. The law is manifestly unequal, and one African man in two can expect to see the inside of a prison each decade. The majority of the population does not even have a formal say in the laws under which it lives, nor is it bound by ties of kinship or historical allegiance to its rulers. Despite this the powder keg has not detonated and clearly if ideological control is weak, physical control must be strong. If all societies are held together by a mixture of consent and coercion, then in South Africa the element of consent must be extremely low and the element of coercion extremely high.[1]

The legal framework for this coercion was described in Section I. However, the core of apartheid is not its laws but the sophisticated machinery that implements them. This machinery consists of a modern bureaucracy backed up by a potent police and military. At least 12 governmental departments (analogous to cabinet level departments in the U.S.) are largely devoted to controlling the life of non-whites. These include: Department of Defence, South African Police, Bureau of State Security, Department of Prisons, Department of Justice, Department of Bantu Adminstration (now called Plural Relations) and Development, Department of Labour, Department of Bantu Education, Department of Indian Affairs, Administration of Coloured Affairs, and Department of Coloured, Rehoboth and Nama Relations.[2]

Such institutions can keep track of 22 million non-white South Africans. They can direct or certify the decisions these individuals make as to residence and employment. They can resettle thousands of Africans in a single administrative swoop. They can effectively isolate and defuse black resistance through harassment, imprisonment, bannings, and exile. This governmental machinery is able to command the behavior of South Africa's blacks because violationg its orders will with high probability result in penalties. Penalties range from small fines to loss of job to jailing or banishment to Bantustans. Over 1000 Africans are prosecuted every day just for pass law violations.[3] Between 1910 and 1973 police fired upon groups of protesting blacks over 30 times.[4] And during the summer 1976 riots alone several hundred protestors were killed.[5]

Vast material resources and the most up-to-date technology available fuel the apartheid machine. According to the *Wall Street Journal*, "The cost of apartheid is immense . . . "[6] In 1976-77 over 20% of the national budget went to supporting the state security apparatus, police, prisons and defense forces.[7] To this figure could be added the cost of influx control, removal and resettlements, political institutions like the Urban Bantu Councils, provision of separate facilities, Bantu administration, and other portions of the budgets of those departments named above. The influx control laws by themselves annually take 112,825,237 rand to administer.[8] A significant part of this money goes for sophisticated equipment like computers and telecommunications gear that is the skeleton of any contemporary bureaucracy.

Apartheid is truly the child of an advanced industrial society. Ironically, it is the very wealth produced by black labor under conditions of extreme exploitation that makes continued white domination possible. Only with the economic surplus and particular products which an economy like South Africa's produces could a system of domination such as apartheid be sustained. But the South African economy has not developed in isolation. Western European and American business has been making critical contributions all along the way—financing and equipping the economy, nurturing the growth of a strong police and military, and guaranteeing the tacit political support of Western governments.

The Foreign Factor

Beginning with the Dutch East India Company in the 17th century, continuing in the form of British mining capital in the late 19th century, and culminating in Western European and United States manufacturing capital in the last three decades, foreign investment in South Africa has been a major engine for economic growth.[9] As an independent economic entity South Africa would never have gotten to where it is today, nor could it go very far in the future. The South African Reserve Bank stated this clearly in 1972:

> In the long run, South Africa has to a large extent been dependent on foreign capital for developmental purposes . . . it is still highly dependent on foreign capital, particularly risk capital, to achieve a relatively high rate of growth.[10]

During the period of economic take-off in South Africa after World War II, 1946-1950, the average net inflow of foreign capital amounted to nearly 40% of gross domestic investment.[11] The average annual inflow of new capital between 1965 and 1969, years of especially rapid growth, was more than $308 million—about one-tenth of gross domestic investment over those years.[12] Between 1970 and 1976, the average net inflow was approximately R800 million (about $1 billion per year), an average contribution of over 13% annual to gross domestic investment.[13] In some of these years, new foreign capital inflows accounted for extraordinarily high proportions of gross domestic investment: 19% in 1971 and 23.2% in 1975. (For purposes of comparison, the average net inflow of foreign capital into the United States contributes between 1% and 2% of gross domestic investment.)

These figures refer only to new foreign capital brought into South Africa each year, and severely understate the total contribution of foreign business to gross domestic investment; they exclude the part of profits foreign corporations make in South Africa and then re-invest within that country. For example, from 1973 to 1975, the shares, premiums and undistributed profits from foreign firms in South Africa totalled more than $5 billion, with most reinvested there.[14] In many years these retained earnings plowed back into the South African economy will equal or exceed the amount of new foreign capital flowing in from outside the country. In such cases the total foreign contribution to gross domestic investment will be double the figures cited above.

In 1976 the total stock of foreign investment in South Africa amounted to over R20 billion as compared to R2.8 billion in 1956.[15] At the end of the 1960's the official Franzen Commission indicated that 40% of South African manufacturing was controlled by foreign interests.[16] Moreover, it has been estimated that about 80% of South Africa's private industrial production is under foreign control or influence.[17]

South Africa's dependence on a steady inflow of foreign capital is also reflected in the country's balance of payments situation. Balance of payments refers to the flow of commodities and money going in and out of a country through trade and investment. South Africa must have enough foreign exchange to cover the cost of the goods it imports from other countries. Foreign exchange comes from exporting goods or obtaining foreign capital through attracting direct investment and bank loans. If these sources fall short, the difference can be made up by selling gold reserves.

The vigor of the South African economy is closely tied to its balance of payment status. While South Africa ranks 23rd in total output, it is one of the top 15 trading countries in the world. Between 1959 and 1968, its exports and imports together were equal to 51.6% of the gross domestic product, and in 1976 were equal to more than one-fourth of its GDP.[18] In nearly every year over the past three decades, South Africa's imports have exceeded her exports. Between 1961 and 1969, total imports increased by 100% and exports by only 50%.[19] Thus South Africa has been unable to finance on its own through export trade the imports which its industrial growth requires. The country can bridge some of this gap by selling its gold reserves; yet the depletion of reserves threatens the value of South African currency and the status of South Africa in the world monetary system. It is a last resort.

According to Colin Legum, a long-time analyst of South Africa, this balance of payments situation reveals a fundamental weakness in the country's economy, a weakness for which American and other capital has effectively compensated:

> The root cause of South Africa's economic problems lies, on the broadest level, in the inability of its production process to develop sufficiently to be able to supply its industries with modern machinery and equipment. This results in South Africa having to import most of its machine requirements. From 1959-1974 machinery and transport equipment were the biggest imports, while their share of total imports rose from 36% in 1959 to 48% in 1972. These requirements have to be paid for by either an influx of foreign capital or by an expansion of exports.[20]

Indeed, foreign capital has filled the void in nearly every post-war year except for the early 1960's when there was a net capital outflow due to

41

recessionary economic conditions and political turmoil following the Sharpville massacre.[21] For example, in 1971 when the balance of payments deficit was just over R1 billion, more than 80% of the deficit was made up by an R818 million inflow of foreign capital. Similarly in 1974, over 90% of a R1 billion deficit was compensated for by inflows of foreign capital.[22] The Bureau of Economic Research at the prestigious Stellenbosch University in South Africa has estimated that well over R1 billion in foreign capital will be needed annually in the near future if the levels of gold and other foreign reserves are to be maintained.[23]

It is important to remember that the flow of foreign capital in to South Africa represents a host of commodities crucial to the industrial infrastructure. These investments are not just clerical entries in the country's capital and balance of payments statements. As Sean Gervasi wrote in a recent U.N. publication on foreign investment in South Africa,

> The importation of capital is of more than purely quantitative importance. In many instances capital inflows are in fact the finance for purchasing sophisticated goods, especially machinery, which cannot be made in South Africa . . . What this means is that foreign 'capital' cannot be replaced simply by finding new sources of finance in South Africa. These capital imports are in fact irreplaceable. The figure for net capital imports is to some extent a measure of the volume of irreplaceable commodities necessary for sustaining economic growth.[24]

Research by British economist John Suckling has attempted to quantify the importance of these "irreplaceable commodities." He has estimated that about 60% of the growth in South Africa's gross domestic product between 1957 and 1972 could be ascribed to "technological change," two-thirds of which was the result of new technology entering the country through foreign investment.[25]

Not all this technology is embodied in machines and equipment; much of it is knowledge and expertise. Following a visit to South Africa in 1970, American scientist Philip Boffey wrote,

> While government and industry realize that research is an important component of economic growth, they also recognize that South Africa is too small to obtain a position on many frontiers of economically valuable science and technology. Therefore, connections with foreign science and technology are vigorously encouraged, generously subsidized when necessary, and diligently exploited for the benefit of the South African economy.[26]

One sector of the South African economy which has substantially benefited from the United States and Western Europe is the nuclear industry.[27] Another beneficiary has been the arms industry. In May 1968 the Armaments Development and Production Corporation (ARMSCOR) was established by a R100 million grant from the government. Its mission has been the nurturing of a domestic capacity for South Africa's weapons needs. Part of the justification for founding ARMSCOR was the need to more efficiently involve foreign capital in the military-industrial complex:

> In introducing the legislation creating ARMSCOR, the Minister of Defense said that a number of overseas firms had approached the government to suggest the joint establishment with South African concerns of armament factories in the Republic. The government welcomed these initiatives on the ground that technical 'know-how' would be available and South Africa's research costs correspondingly reduced. The new corporation would, it was claimed, facilitate links between local and overseas producers.[28]

This strategy has in fact been successful, with South Africa now virtually self-sufficient in production of all but the most sophisticated arms.

American Investment in South Africa

United States banks and corporations rank high in terms of the foreign contribution to South Africa's economy. After Britain, America is the largest foreign investor in South Africa. It has channeled capital to that country through both direct and indirect investment. The former is represented by U.S. corporations participating in wholly or partially owned subsidiaries in South Africa, while the latter primarily consists of American bank loans.

American companies have at least $1.665 billion of direct investments in South Africa, comprising 17% of all direct foreign investments there.[29] In addition, U.S. banks have over $2 billion in outstanding loans to South Africa, accounting for 33% of all loan claims against the country.[30] These are minimum totals; in a study for the UN Professor Lee Friedman reports:

> Estimates of American investment in South Africa tend to minimize the totals. For years they exempted investment of Canadian corporations wholly or principally owned by business and financial enterprises in the United States. Ford of Canada is a noteworthy example. More recent estimates have neglected to take into account American investment in British and West European companies and banks that have invested substantial capital in manufacturing, processing, and refining plants and commercial operations in South Africa. Therefore, to estimate American [direct] investments in the Republic in excess of two billion dollars in 1977 is reasonable.[31]

Nor do these figures suggest the special qualitative importance of U.S. investment, its post-war rise, its concentration in major sectors of the economy, or its domination by a significant but limited number of strategic firms.

Since World War II, U.S. direct investment in South Africa has snowballed. In 1950 it had a book value of $140 million. Seven years later that figure had more than doubled, and by 1961 had risen to $353 million. This amount more than doubled by 1970, to $750 million, and doubled again in the next five years to reach $1.56 billion in 1975. This represents more than a 1000% increase between 1950 and 1975.[32]

American investment has increasingly been directed into the most rapidly growing sectors of the economy. In 1959, 34% of U.S. direct investment was in manufacturing, 27% in mining and almost nothing in petroleum. By 1970, over 50% was in manufacturing, 10% in mining and 25% in petroleum.[33] Manufacturing contributed a larger proportion of South Africa's Gross Domestic Product (22.1% in 1974) than any other sector. Its growth has in part been promoted by American expertise and technology.[34]

The U.S. corporations involved in South Africa include some of the largest multinationals in the world. Although there are over 320 American firms operating in South Africa today, a relative few control most of the U.S. investment. As of 1973, three-fourths of U.S. direct investment in South Africa was in the hands of 12 companies.[35] Four of these—Mobil, Caltex, Ford and General Motors—are probably among the top 25 non-mining corporations in the country.[36] Because of the size and nature of their activities, these and other American subsidiaries play a major role in the South African economy. An examination of their operations in some of the most strategic and dynamic sectors of the economy—petroleum, motor vehicles, computers, mining, and high technology and heavy engineering—illustrates the U.S. corporate contribution to apartheid.

Petroleum

Oil in South Africa is imported, refined and marketed by six multinational firms. Three of these are American—Caltex, Mobil and Exxon—and they control about 44% of that country's petroleum products market.[37] Both Caltex, a jointly owned subsidiary of Texaco and Standard Oil of California, and Mobil have South African refineries, and each has about half of this market share with Exxon comparatively insignificant. As of 1977 Caltex had about $200 million invested in South Africa and Mobil had $333 million.[38] Caltex is currently involved in a $134 million expansion which will increase South Africa's refining capacity by 11%. $100 million of this new investment has come from company funds outside South Africa.[39] The *Financial Mail* has commented that,

Without the massive resources of the big international oil companies, applied through their South African subsidiaries, the oil industry in the

44

Republic would not have built into a R700 million business. A stake in the South African market is of great benefit to the oil "majors," for it is a lucrative one and ripe for expansion. In return they have put a vast amount of capital and know-how into the country.[40]

Petroleum supplies about 25% of South Africa's energy. Almost all of this goes into transportation. 80% of imported crude oil is converted into fuel: 36% of this for industry, 36% for private motorists, 11% for agriculture, 10% for commerce and 5% for aviation. The chemical industry represents the other major consumer of crude oil, employing it as a key ingredient in the production of plastics, asphalt, fertilizer, and other synthetics.[41]

South Africa relies almost entirely on imported oil for its petroleum needs. In the words of a managing director of the Industrial Development Corporation, "dependence on imported fuel is one of South Africa's most vulnerable points."[42] There are no domestic sources of oil except for an oil-from-coal plant, SASOL 1, which satisfies about 8% of the country's petroleum needs.

Because of the strategic nature of oil in South Africa, relations between the government and multinational oil companies have been extremely close. The government announced in 1967 that the petroleum companies would have to: 1) make their refineries available for processing crude products from any source, when excess capacity is available, 2) give South African institutions and individuals the opportunity to buy shares in the local operation, 3) ensure that the major proportion of their earnings remained in South Africa to finance the future expansion of the industry, 4) be prepared to produce specialized petroleum and oil products required for strategic and other logistical reasons irrespective of the commercial potential.[43]

The intent and impact of such regulations have been to make American oil companies in South Africa serve the economic, military and political interests of their host country. The Investor Responsibility Research Center reports that according to an official of the South African embassy, "there is a continuous consultation between oil companies and the government on such matters as projected demand and prices, that the relationship between private oil concerns and the government is very close, and that one could assume that arrangements had been made to meet government needs."[44] The U.S. firms are cooperative since the government has control through a variety of regulations, and an oil company can only get a competitive edge through courting the state's favor. For example, Caltex and Mobil have engaged in substantial oil exploration within South Africa and its coastal waters. Even though the economic payoff to such activity is very doubtful, it is something which the government views quite positively.[45]

Details of oil company collaboration with the South African police and military remain unknown. It is known that in 1975 oil refined by Caltex for the government accounted for 6.8% of its total sales.[46] In response to demands for more information, Caltex's U.S. parent company has said,

> Caltex South Africa has advised that under South African law it cannot disclose information concerning its obligations in regard to the distribution of its products in South Africa.[47]

Caltex has also stated that under South African law it cannot commit itself to not supplying the military:

> Further, we have been advised that it would be a crime under South Africa's laws were Caltex South Africa to undertake a commitment not to supply petroleum products to the Government of South Africa, whether for use by the South African military or any other branch of the South African government.[48]

The clearest statement of the strategic importance of American oil companies in South Africa has been made by Mobil itself. In response to requests by the United Church of Christ for information pertaining to Mobil's alleged circumvention of economic sanctions against Rhodesia, Mobil South Africa obtained the following opinion from its law firm. Under the South African Official Secrets Act, Mobile cannot provide:

> Information about the details of transactions concerning oil in southern Africa . . . such information being sought for disclosure to the Federal authorities—that is, to the United States Government.

> The State would in any event be able to tender evidence that such information should be likely to be directly or indirectly useful to an enemy. Oil supplies are the very lifeblood of the army, navy and air force, and information in regard to the sources thereof, refining, storage, reserves and distribution, are of the utmost strategic importance to the State. It can accordingly readily be envisaged that the South African Minister of Defense would allege that disclosure of such information to the Federal authorities is likely to be useful to an enemy.[49]

If the American oil companies have a share of the military petroleum market at least as large as their share of the general petroleum market in South Africa, then they are supplying nearly one-half of "the very lifeblood of the army, navy and air force."

Besides these routinely critical services that U.S. petroleum firms provide to South Africa, they are active in other parts of the larger region. Through their South African subsidiaries, Mobil and Caltex are helping to break the economic boycott of Rhodesia imposed by the UN Security Council in May 1968. Documentary evidence released during the past

46

years shows that these two companies, along with Total, Shell and British Petroleum, have assisted Rhodesia in importing all the oil it needs. They do not sell petroleum directly to that country but instead through intermediary concerns in South Africa. Mobil referred to this scheme as a "paper chase."[50]

The sanction-breaking activities of American oil companies go beyond their Rhodesian ploys. Several Arab oil exporting countries have voluntarily stopped supplying South Africa with crude, in line with calls for such a boycott by the Organization of African Unity (OAU). According to the Interfaith Center on Corporate Responsibility,

> Caltex has already played a major role, together with other multinationals oil companies, in supplying oil to South Africa in defiance of the Middle East suppliers. The mechanism by which this is done by Caltex emerged publicly during the course of a tax case involving the company in South Africa. It appears that Caltex Oil South Africa, Caltex United Kingdom and the U.K. based Caltex Services are all wholly-owned subsidiaries of the U.S. Caltex Petroleum Corporation. Caltex S.A. obtains suplies of crude oil primarily from Caltex Services. In turn, Caltex S.A. sells a certain amount of petroleum products, and supplies certain services to Caltex U.K. and Caltex Services. Caltex S.A. informs the British company about a year in advance of its requirements, and Caltex U.K. then purchases the supplies directly from the producing country and arranges for them to be loaded, usually at ports in the Persian Gulf. Caltex S.A. then pays Caltex U.K. in sterling. By this means, the producing country has no means of knowing that the real destination is South Africa.[51]

The multinationals can also execute a complicated series of swaps to allocate more oil to South Africa from Iran, the one petroleum producing country that is still making significant above-board exports to the white regime.[52]

Motor Vehicles

Like the oil industry, motor vehicle manufacturing in South Africa is dominated by foreign multinationals—American, Japanese and German. The American firms—General Motors, Ford and Chrysler (with a 24.9% interest in a joint venture with SA Anglo-American)—control at least one-third of the market.[53] As of 1977 General Motors had approximately $220 million invested in the Republic, Ford had $254 million and Chrysler's affiliate, Sigma, had about $117 million.[54] Total capital investment in the industry in 1970 was $430 million; two-thirds of this amount was invested since 1960, and of this, over 60% came from the U.S. manufacturers.[55] Both GM and Ford operations in the RSA appear quite large relative to the size of South African corporations. GM South Africa ranked 34th in

47

employment and 17th in total assets and sales among the top 100 industrial companies listed in a 1975 survey by the *Financial Mail.*[56]

The automotive industry stands as a keystone of the South African economy. In 1968 a publication of South Africa's Standard Bank stated:

> The motor vehicle industry is one of the most dynamic forces in the expanding South African economy. From a core of vehicle manufacture and assembly its influence extends to most manufacturing industries . . . Its future pattern of growth will affect the whole economy.[57]

By 1970 the motor vehicle industry was contributing 7% of South Africa's entire Gross National Product and accounting for 14% of total investment in the economy.[58]

Because the automotive sector has such substantial linkages with other major sectors of the economy, incorporates a sophisticated technology, and produces a valuable product, the government of South Africa views it as a strategic resource. In the late 1960's a leading South African economist stated that the automobile manufacturing industry was " . . . the government's chosen instrument for achieving the crucial sophistication of industrialization over the next decade, when gold mining is expected to decline in significance."[59]

To maximize the contribution of the auto companies to South Africa's economic, political and military strength, the government embarked on a "local content" program in 1962. It required that increasingly large proportions of the components going into vehicles assembled in South Africa be produced within the country rather than imported. This so-called local content had to be at least 55% by 1969 and 65% by 1976.[60] Enforcement of the program was accomplished through excise duty rebates and restrictions on importing components. The goals of local content have been five-fold: promotion of a specialized and strong domestic engineering sector which would fill a major void in the national industrial structure, conservation of limited and over-taxed foreign exchange, creation of a potential export industry, macro-economic stimulation of the entire economy, and expansion of military independence.[61]

Foreign automobile manufacturers in South Africa have responded vigorously to this government strategy, and the local content requirements have been met. According to plan the auto components industries within South Africa have prospered, with investment in components firms increasing from $18.6 million in 1960 to $210 million in 1970.[62] Much of this has been in steel, rubber, and glass. The first car to be designed and developed within the Republic—the Ranger—was the off-spring of General Motors.[63]

More direct contributions by Ford and General Motors to the South African security apparatus can be identified as well. In 1973 Ford reported that its sales to the government, including the police and military, had amounted to about 1% of total sales in South Africa over the preceding decade; this figure represents about $2 million worth of vehicles annually.[64] It is known that Ford has sold 17 transport buses, among other things, to the South African Defence Forces.[65] The National Council of Churches' Corporate Information Center reports that "Many GM vehicles are used by the South African police for general activities, including transportation of prisoners to jail."[66] In May 1968, a GM spokesman in Detroit confirmed that GM South Africa Ltd. had supplied trucks to the government for "defense force purposes." He said:

> We don't make military vehicles as such, but they (the South Africans) adapt them for whatever purposes they want.[67]

In addition to current sales to the security forces, American auto companies in South Africa play an important role in the contingency planning of the military. Besides the onimous precedent of GM plants in Germany being converted to production for the Nazi military machine,[68] Ford and GM factories in South Africa were used for military production during World War II and could, if necessary, be converted again.

> In times of emergency or war each plant could be turned over rapidly to the production of weapons and other strategic requirements for the defense of South Africa.[69]

As major military contractors in the United States, both firms have enormous experience and expertise to draw upon, including the production of tanks, rifles, engines for military aircraft, jeeps, grenade launchers, missiles and communications systems for anti-guerrilla warfare.

A recently-revealed, secret riot plan further points up the dangerous possibilities. In a contingency memorandum prepared at the request of the parent company, GM officials in South Africa said:

> In the event that a national emergency is declared, there is little doubt that control of GM South Africa's facilities, already designated a national Key-Point Industry, would be taken over by an arm of the Ministry of Defence and its production capabilities integrated into the national industrial efforts.[70]

The plan also revealed that GM and other strategic industries would be protected in emergencies by a Citizen Force Commando system. GM plant personnel with military training were encouraged "by the authorities" to volunteer for local commando units.

Computers

South Africa has no major domestic computer firms. The market is dominated by several American companies—including International Business Machines, National Cash Register, Burroughs, Control Data Corporation, Univac-Sperry Rand, Honeywell, Hewlett Packard—and Britain's giant International Computers Ltd. In 1974 private corporations and the government in South Africa had about 1000 computers in use.[71] It has been estimated that United States firms control about 70% of this market, with most of the rest handled by ICL.[72] IBM stands as the single largest supplier and servicer of data-processing equipment in the country; estimates of its market share range from 38% to 50%.[73] A survey by *Management* (a SA business magazine) in late 1974 was able to identify two-thirds of South Africa's computer installations; 240 of these were leased or purchased from IBM. At that time NCR and Burroughs each accounted for about 100 computers in the country.[74]

Like any other advanced, industrialized economy, South Africa could not function without the employment of sophisticated data processing devices. The managing director of Burroughs South Africa, C. Cotton, said in March 1971:

> We're entirely dependent on the U.S. The economy would grind to a halt without access to the computer technology of the West. No bank could function; the government couldn't collect its money and couldn't account for it; business couldn't operate; payrolls could not be paid. Retail and wholesale marketing and related services would be disrupted.[75]

IBM computers are being used by many of the leading business institutions in South Africa, including the Johannesburg Stock Exchange, Chamber of Mines, United Building Society, Anglo-American Corporation, and African Explosive and Chemical Industries.[76] In its promotional statement IBM says, "Keeping up with our South African businessmen isn't easy . . . We do our best to help the South African businessman grow."[77] The strong demand for electronic data-processing equipment in South Africa is in part the direct result of apartheid. Limitations on the employment of non-whites in salaried, administrative jobs puts a premium on automating such tasks. In this sense, U.S. computer firms are helping to solve the skilled white labor problem.

The assistance which American computer companies give to the South African government is at least as crucial to maintaining apartheid as the administrative services they provide in the private sector. At least one-third of all IBM's business in South Africa is with the government.[78] U.S. marketed and serviced computers are in use in at least 18 government agencies, including the following:[79]

50

- *Department of Defence*—3 IBM 370/158s and 2 370/145s. Reportedly used for "Personnel, financial and stock control."
- *Department of Prisons*—1 IBM 360/20. Reportedly used in "financial" applications.
- *Atomic Energy Board*—1IBM 370/155, 1 CDC 1700, 1 HP 2115, 3 HP 2114, and 1 Varian 602/L. IBM says its computer is used for "administrative applications such as controlling the industrial use of radioactive materials and providing a library and information retrieval function."
- *Council for Scientific and Industrial Research*—1 IBM 370/158, 1 IBM 370/135, 1 IBM 370/115 used for "General scientific and engineering applications." Several Varian computers are used for "various departments of scientific work." (Manufacturers tend not to mention that the Council is responsible for overseeing all military, as well as civilian, research.)
- *Department of Interior*—2 IBM 370/158s used for "population registration system" for Coloured, Asians and whites known as the "Book of Life."
- *Armaments Board*—1NCR C100, 1 HP 2116. Use is unknown. The Armaments Board "Controls the manufacture, acquisition, development and supply of armaments."
- *ESCOM* (government controlled and managed Electricity Supply Commission)—1 IBM 370/158, 1 IBM 370/145, 3 IBM 370/135, 3 CDC 1700, 1 CDC 6400, several IBM 3/10. The IBM machines are used for "accounting and project management in the distribution of electric power."

It is the position of IBM (and presumably other American computer firms in South Africa) that their equipment is used in normal administrative functions; that all computer sales and services are consistent with U.S. law and U.N. regulation; and that they "know of no use of any IBM computers down there that directly support any part of apartheid."[80] However, given the use of IBM and other U.S. computers by the South African government, it would be more correct to say that American computers "down there" give substantial support to apartheid.

Even routine functions such as accounting and inventory control have an important strategic dimension when they are being performed for the South African armed forces or prisons. The South African Defence Forces, the Armaments Board, and the Department of Prisons all have key roles in the apartheid machine. The Defence Forces secure the borders from insurgency and represent a second line of defense against black insurrection within the country. They have recently fought against guerrillas in both Angola and Namibia. The Armaments Board has effectively shouldered the job of equipping the armed forces with modern weapons in the face of a partial arms embargo against South Africa. And

51

South Africa has one of the largest daily prison populations in the world, many prisoners being pass law offenders. American computers help these institutions do their job of preserving white dominance as efficiently as possible. Keeping track of military personnel is not the same as keeping track of deposits in a bank. Stock control has a special significance when the inventory includes implements of war.

Many computer uses appear to go beyond anything which could be called routine. Such a case is the employment of IBM equipment in computerizing the "Book of Life."[81] This document represents for Coloureds and Asians in South Africa what the passbook is for blacks. It contains an assortment of information about the individual and must be carried at all times. The Group Areas Act, which controls the residency and movements of Coloureds and Asians, could not be enforced without the storage of individual records on sophisticated computers like those IBM provides. Computerization means that the appropriate South African authorities have Book of Life information about millions of people at their fingertips. IBM was outbid for the African passbook computer by ICL in 1965.[82]

The several U.S. computers being used by the sensitive Council on Scientific and Industrial Research are also noteworthy. CSIR has been publicly cited for its contribution to the technological advances that are making South Africa self-sufficient in strategic arms production, e.g, the development and manufacture of Crotale missiles.[83] In regard to the Control Data Corporation computers which the CSIR rents, a report to the Washington, D.C. city government points out that "*South Africa Progress 1972,* a government publication, boasts of CSIR's aviation research which has given South Africa the ability to manufacture three types of fighter-bombers. Appearing on the same page that notes these aviation research achievements are several pictures of wind tunnel studies. CSIR utilizes two CDC computers. One is used in wind tunnel research."[84] The 360/65 computer rented by CSIR from IBM is the same type of computer used by the U.S. Air Force to manage electronic warfare during the Vietnam War.[85]

Police departments in South Africa are very interested in the potential of computers. At a law enforcement seminar in Johannesburg three years ago, Sperry Rand made a major presentation to 100 top ranking police and provincial administration officials. The firm displayed one of their computer systems to show the ease of information retrieval and its advantages to law enforcement.[86]

Mining

The American stake in mining has been growing over the last one and a half decades. In 1960, only one-sixth of all foreign direct investment in this sector of the South African economy came from U.S. companies. By 1976 the proportion had grown to one-fourth. As of 1973 this direct American investment in mining amounted to $138 million, a 100% increase over 1968 levels.[87] Moreover, these figures understate the total U.S. involvement in mining since more than two-thirds of that investment is not direct but indirect—through mining house shares traded on the Johannesburg Stock Exchange.[88] The London *Economist* has estimated that U.S. capital owns 33% of all South African gold mining shares.[89]

South Africa's mineral resources are vast. The country is the world's leading gold producer, supplying about 80% of the non-communist world's gold. South Africa and Namibia together yield more diamond gems than any other country. South Africa has 75% of the world's chrome reserves and 33% of its uranium reserves. In addition, the country has enormous deposits of coal, platinum, vanadium and many other minerals and metals.[90]

Exploitation of these natural deposits has stimulated the entire economy, beginning with the primary industrializatoin of South Africa induced by the early mining of gold and diamonds in the late 19th century. Mining has directly led to the formation of local industries which produce heavy engineering equipment and process mineral and metal extractions.[91]

Of particular importance in recent years has been the foreign exchange brought into South Africa through mineral exports. For example, in 1975 (a typical year) exports of minerals earned R3,540 million in foreign exchange. This was over 60% of all export-earned foreign exchange.[92]

In 1972 the *New York Times* reported that, "Some of America's largest mining corporations—United States Steel, The Phelps Dodge Corporation, and Newmont Mining—are stepping up their operations in South Africa, and more American companies are entering the South African quest for minerals."[93] The most important U.S. mining companies in South Africa include Union Carbide, Newmont Mining, Phelps Dodge and Kennecott. A summary of their operation suggests the overall role of U.S. companies in mining.

Union Carbide produces 20% of South African chrome.[94] In 1976 it opened a new $50 million ferrochrome plant in partnership with a local firm, the General Mining and Finance Corporation.[95] Commenting on this and similar advances in the chrome industry, a South African government publication recently noted that, "This investment confirms South Africa's stable political environment and points to an economic and legal climate attractive to foreign investors."[96] Union Carbide is also involved in vanadium mining and smelting, the latter yielding an alloy never before produced out the United States. The *Financial Gazette* reported that this process "should earn considerable foreign exchange" for South Africa.[97]

Newmont holds 57.5% of O'okiep Copper Company, 28.6% of Palabora Mining Company and 11.8% of Highveld Steel, all in South Africa, and 29.6% of the Tsumeb Corporation in Namibia. Palabora is the largest copper operation in South Africa and O'okiep the second largest. Newmont's share of these investments is worth over $120 million.[98]

Phelps Dodge is a fairly new entrant into South African mining, having first invested in South Africa during 1970, but it already has subsidiaries there with total assets of $25 million.[99] Phelps Dodge owns one of the most promising mineral deposits in all of South Africa—a major lead, copper, zinc and silver concentration at Aggenneys in the northwestern part of Cape Province. It is a partner in a $191 million joint venture with Gold Fields of South Africa to develop these deposits.[100] The Minister of Mines has said that exploitation of these Phelps Dodge properties could produce metals worth more than $1.4 billion per year.[101]

Kennecott Copper Corporation has investments in South African mining through its two-thirds ownership of Quebec Iron and Titanium (QIT). QIT is currently involved in a massive ilmenite mining and smelting complex near Richards Bay, a port currently being developed on the eastern coast of South Africa. The operation will produce both iron and titanium dioxide. QIT has committed itself to providing $114 million out of $290 million required to capitalize the project. Remaining capital will come from the government Industrial Development Corporation and the Union Corporation, a private mining and finance company. Both controlling interest and management of the Richards Bay operation will rest with QIT. According to the fact-finding Investor Responsibility Research Center, "Were QIT to leave the project, it is quite possible that the Richards Bay Project would be indefinitely delayed. The project requires foreign investment from QIT but also is dependent on the company's technology."[102]

Other American-based companies involved in South African mining include American Metal Climax (copper), Alcan Aluminum, Kaiser Aluminum, U.S. Steel and King Resources.[103]

High Technology and Heavy Engineering

Virtually all American firms in South Africa not located in motor vehicle manufacturing, oil refining, computers or mining, operate in high technology and/or heavy engineering industries. They manufacture intermediate, capital goods which are then used by other manufacturers in the country. They provide the implements or expertise necessary for the construction of major public and private works projects. They produce goods for final consumption which are of recent invention and make use of complicated production processes.

The best example of such a United States subsidiary in South Africa is

General Electric. South African General Electric Company has supplied 80% of the diesel locomotives currently in service with the state-run South African railways.[104] In 1976 S.A.G.E. contracted to provide 40 new locomotives for the Sishen-Saldanha project—a major railway and port development designed for the export of huge new iron deposits now being mined.[105] The rail system managed by SAR and traversed by G.E. locomotives is vital to the economy. According to South African economist Sandra van der Merwe, "Long distance transport is exclusively the province of the South African Railways (SAR)—apart from a particular range of goods which go by road for certain reasons."[106]

South African G.E. sells and services motor control equipment to the government corporation ISCOR, a concern meeting 72% of the country's iron and steel requirements. This equipment enables automated, round-the-clock control of ISCOR machinery and plants. The development of an efficient, powerful iron and steel industry has been a main component of government plans for achieving industrial and military self-sufficiency.[107]

Only adverse political reaction in the U.S. prevented General Electric from providing a nuclear reactor system to ESCOM, the South African state Electricity Supply Commission. A multi-million dollar deal between G.E. and ESCOM fell through when the Export-Import Bank refused to finance the sale and Congress began to voice criticism. The company lobbied the EX-IM Bank to change its policy on South Africa lending but was unsuccessful.[108]

In addition to these activities, South African G.E. manufactures calrods, capacitators, magnet wires, switchgears and controls, freezers, refrigerators, washers and housewares, and constructed 130 control relay panels for the South African terminal of the power grid from the Cabora Bassa Dam.[109]

Other notable American firms in high technology and heavy engineering are (by sub-sector):

Agricultural, mining and construction equipment: John Deere had approximately $30 million invested in South Africa as of 1977. The company manufacturers and assembles tractors and tractor parts, chisel ploughs, subsoilers, etc.[110] Caterpillar Tractor had $14.5 in its subsidiary in 1975. The firm processes parts for construction equipment and facilitates local procurement of replacement parts for Caterpillar machinery."[111] Dresser Industries manufactures hydraulic mining machinery, road maintenance equipment, and petroleum service station equipment. The amount which Dresser has invested in its subsidiary is unknown, but with 1120 employees it is probably among the top twenty-five American companies in South Africa.[112] Baker International Group of the U.S. just put R2 million into a factory complex for its subsidiary Reed Tool Company. It will make rotary blast-hole drill bits for mining which heretofore had been imported. According to a Reed spokesperson, "This will result in considerable saving in foreign exchange for South Africa and will make the local mining industry less dependent on overseas supply."[113] Norton Co. has subsidiaries in South Africa manufacturing hand tools, grinding wheels and buffing and polishing equipment.[114]

Rubber: United States and British firms dominate the rubber industry. Goodyear and Firestone are two of the top three firms in this sector.[115] Goodyear's subsidiary had $58 million worth of assets as of 1977.[116] South Africa Railways, responsible for the country's large public truck transport system, is one of its largest customers, as are other governmental agencies. The company is a prime manufacturer of large conveyor belts used in mining, and in 1975 completed a $10 million plant built for this purpose.[117] Firestone had an estimated $25-$30 million in its South African operations in 1973. Like Goodyear, it makes a whole range of car, truck and tractor tires and tubes, retread and repair, materials, and rubber products such as conveyors, hoses and V-belts.[118] In 1972, B.F. Goodrich set up a R20 million plant near Durban in partnership with Japanese concerns.[119]

Electronics: Motorola has several million dollars invested in its subsidiary. It manufactures communications equipment, electronic measuring, controlling and recording equipment, and car alternators. A major contract between Motorola and ISCOR was announced by the South African papers in June 1974:

> A R4 million contract for the supply and commissioning of a complete microwave project . . . awarded by ISCOR to Motorola, Inc. of Chicago. . . . the project team will include South Africans and a specialized engineering staff from the parent company.

The major customer in South Africa for Motorola's mobile two-way radio sets is the South African police.[120]

ITT recently merged its subsidiary, Standard Telephone and Cables, into South African-owned Allied Technologies, which is now 36.3% ITT held.[121] Standard Telephone and Cable (STC), one of South Africa's biggest electrical manufacturing firms, supplies communications equipment for the police and Simonstown Naval Base, and many of its employees must have security clearances.[122] In 1968 the *Financial Mail* termed the electronics industry "a key to an up-to-date defence force." [123]

Photography and Copying: Kodak has $6.5 million invested in South Africa. The firm processes and distributes film and equipment, controlling a large share of the photography business.[124] DuPont provided technical assistance for the construction of a film finishing plant recently completed in Johannesburg. When fully operational, the plant could save South Africa R3 million annually in foreign exchange.[125] Xerox owns 75% of Rank Xerox and has 51% of the voting power in that firm. Rank Xerox, with assets of $14 million, holds approximately a one-third share of the copying market.[126]

Miscellaneous: Allis Chalmers, in cooperation with other U.S. firms, built the SAFARI I research and test reactor at Pelindaba, where South Africa's capability for enriching uranium is being developed. Journalists Tami Hultman and Reed Kramer report:

> By enriching as well as mining the mineral, South Africa will multiply both its earnings and its political punch. Moreover, as the only major uranium producer and the only uranium enriching nation which has not signed the Treaty on the Nonproliferation of Nuclear Weapons, South Africa retains an unparalleled freedom of action in the competitive and strategic nuclear field.[127]

Another sophisticated construction project is now being managed by Fluor Corporation of Los Angeles. Fluor is the main contractor for the building of SASOL II, the coal-to-gas conversion plant which upon completion in 1981 will satisfy about 25% of South Africa's oil-based fuel needs.[128] This $2.2 billion "megaproject" represents a strategic technology transfer critically important to South Africa's ability to meet the threat of international oil sanctions. Philips Petroleum owns one-half of Phillips Carbon Black, the country's only producer of carbon black, a key ingredient in binding rubber.[129] Minnesota Mining and Manufacturing has $6.5 million invested in its subsidiary. It manufactures and/or distributes tape, graphic and plastic products.[130]

Banking and Finance

So far the discussion has concerned American **direct** investment in the South African economy—investment where a U.S.-based corporation set-up a wholly or partially-owned subsidiary operation. But an even greater amount of American capital goes to South Africa in the form of **indirect** investment. This consists primarily of loans that U.S. banks or their subsidiaries make to South African governmental agencies, businesses, or commercial banks.

About one-third of all loan claims against South Africa are held by American banks or their overseas branches. As of August 1976, these financial institutions had over $2 billion in outstanding loans to South Africa, double the amount 18 months earlier. In October 1976 a new $110 million loan was made to South Africa by U.S. banks.[131]

The bulk of American loans to South Africa have been made by Chase Manhattan, Citibank, Manufacturers Hanover Trust, Morgan Guaranty, and Bank of America. Citibank alone has total liabilities of $200 million in South Africa from international loans.[132] Bank of America has at least $180 million in finance extended to the country.[133] Frequently U.S. banks do not loan directly to South Africa on their own but through international consortia like the European-American Banking Corporation.[134]

Several regional banks like Republic National Bank of Dallas and United Virginia Bank participated in loans to South Africa during the early 1970's but have become "gun shy" in recent times. In June 1976 the South African state owned Phosphate Development Corporation (FOSKOR) sought a $30 million loan from these regioal banks but according to the *Financial Mail* they eventually had to go to "traditional friends," the New York banks.[135]

These traditionally friendly U.S. banks, as well as newer American acquaintances, have served the South African status quo quite well. Historically, they have helped to cover chronic balance of payments deficits and to finance government projects. The *Washington Post* last year quoted a local South African financial expert as saying:

> I have this recurring nightmare of Carter calling all the heads of American big banks into a closed meeting and then saying nothing but "We discussed South Africa." They would have us over a big barrel.[136]

Two aspects of U.S. bank loans to South Africa have made them especially vital to maintaining white minority rule. First, they have come primarily during periods in which South Africa has faced serious economic and political instability. Second, the recipients of these loans have generally been prominent institutions of the apartheid government.

In 1960 a peaceful crowd demonstrating against the pass laws was fired upon at Sharpeville. This Sharpeville Massacre, combined with other serious unrest in South Africa during 1960-61, caused a massive flight of foreign capital. Two hundred and seventy-one million dollars was taken out of the country in 1960 and $63 million in early 1961. Foreign reserves dropped from $350 million to $245 million. The net outflow of foreign capital continued through 1964.[137] As South Africa entered a state of emergency, American banks came to the rescue and shored up the economy. Shortly after Sharpeville, financiers in the U.S. put together loans adding up to $150 million. Foremost among these was a $40 million revolving loan offered by a consortium of ten American banks including Chase Manhattan and Citibank.[138]

A malaise no less serious than that following Sharpeville has been gripping the South African economy since late 1974. The country has had to pay continually spiralling prices for its imports, particularly oil. This comes at a time when recession in America and Europe has constricted its export markets. Moreover, the price of gold has been depressed below normal levels, reducing South Africa's ability to bring in foreign exchange. Government expenditure on defense has skyrocketed from R481 million in

1973/74 to R1,350 million in 1976/77; as much as 2/3 of this military spending has gone for imports.[139] The state is concurrently attempting to pursue a $12 billion infrastructure development package designed to enhance the economic and political independence of the country.[140]

Plagued by these economic problems, South Africa has looked toward foreign banks for a bail out. Despite the political crisis of the Angolan War and internal South African unrest since Soweto, U.S. banks have again made their financial resources available. As noted earlier, the amount of their outstanding loans to South Africa doubled between early 1975 and late 1976—a $1 billion increase. Commenting on the ability of the south African government to borrow from foreign banks, the *Financial Mail* stated a month after Soweto:

> . . . a unique feature of the market has been the support of U.S. banks. Apparently more finance has come from this quarter than ever before."[141]

Between January and November, 1976, $777 million was loaned to the South African government, state corporations and private businesses. The majority of these loans were reported after the black township uprisings in June.[142]

A list of recipients of these recent loans reads like a *Who's Who* of South African government corporations. Beginning in the 1920's, these institutions were established to ensure government authority over the most strategic sectors of the economy. They are among the largest economic enterprises in the country.

The Electricity Supply Commission (ESCOM) received a $200 million 5-year loan from Citibank, Chase Manhattan, Manufacturers Hanover, Morgan Guaranty Trust, and Barclays International Ltd.[143] ESCOM operates 21 power stations and provides 86% of the country's power requirements. It is currently involved in an expansion plan intended to meet South Africa's growing energy needs. This plan includes construction of coal-fired, nuclear, and hydro-electric power stations. Approximately $2.9 billion in capital will be required by 1985 to finance the projects.[144] Since ESCOM is restricted by law to diverting no more than 3% of its annual revenues into capital development, it has had to seek foreign loans for its capital expenditures. ESCOM began accepting bids in April 1976 for the building of two nuclear reactors near Cape Town that will cost several hundred million dollars. The $200 million American bank loan made the bidding process easier. for South Africa, even though the contract was ultimately awarded to three French companies. Between 15% and 25% of South Africa's electricity is expected to be generated by nuclear plants by the year 2000.[145]

The Richards Bay titanium mining and smelting project (of which Kennecott is a partner) was the recipient of a $138 million loan from Citibank, Chase Manhattan, Manufacturers HanoverTrust, Barclays and various German banks.[146] This titanium project is part of a larger $1.5

59

billion port and railway development at Richards Bay, 130 miles north of Durban. A $460 million railway line between the coalfields of the eastern Transvaal and the port has already been completed. In addition there will be a phosphoric acid plant, an aluminum smelter, and plants producing pig iron and zircon.[147] The Richards Bay complex and one being built at Saldanha Bay represent two of South Africa's major infrastructure developments.

A $110 million loan was made directly to the South African government by Citibank, Morgan Guaranty Trust and Bank of America.[148] It has helped to cover government deficit spending made necessary by increased defense and security expenditures in a time of lowered tax revenues. This single loan amounted to about 30% of all bank credit that the South African government obtained in the budget year ending June 30, 1977.[149]

The Iron and Steel Corporation (ISCOR) received an $80 million loan from Chase Manhattan, Citibank and Orion.[150] ISCOR needs capital for two major expansions currently in the works. These are a $1.5 billion semi-finished steel plant at Saldanha Bay which will produce for export and a $2.1 billion upgrading of finished steel production capacity.[151]

The Industrial Development Corporation obtained a $25 million loan from the Chase Manhattan Bank in conjunction with the Export-Import Bank. The loan is to help South African business finance imports of American-made plant and equipment. The IDC has been a "mainspring" of South African economic planning, taking over where private capital has been unable to manage its own affairs.[152]

Three other loans are notable. South African Railways received a $75 million loan from a syndicate including Morgan Guaranty.[153] The Phosphate Development Corporation (FOSKOR) successfully sought a $30 million loan from Manufacturers Hanover Trust. Finally, the South African Broadcasting Corporation received a $20 million loan from Citibank.[154]

These loans to state corporations have an impact on the South African situation which transcends the particular industrial projects they capitalize. In testimony before the Senate Subcommittee on African Affairs in September 1976, Timothy Smith of the Interfaith Center on Corporate Responsibility argued:

> If foreign funds were not available to the parastatal agencies, the government itself would have to finance them, thus limiting the cash available for maintaining apartheid. Let us not deceive ourselves that a loan to ESCOM can be simply classified as a loan for electric power. It is a loan directly to an agency of the apartheid government that helps that government balance its overall budget.[155]

While there is no question that indirect investments (bank loans) play a vital role in bolstering the white regime, it is somewhat more difficult to determine whether it is public criticism or the faltering South African economy which accounts for recent policy revisions on the part of some major American banks. In March 1978, Citibank, the second largest bank in the U.S., announced to its stockholders that it would not make loans to the South African government or government-owned enterprises. Citicorp, the bank's parent company, nevertheless made clear that it was opposed to a shareholders' resolution calling for a report on the bank's commitments in South Africa. Ruling out balance-of-payments loans, the corporation's proxy statement echoed the progressive force thesis when it said, "Citicorp is limiting its credit, selectively, to constructive private-sector activities that create jobs and which benefit all South Africans."[156]

No similar justifications have come from top-ranking Bank of America, which maintains it makes loans anywhere in the world. Other banks, including Chase Manhattan and First National of Chicago, seem to share Citibank's caution, and the chairman of Morgan Guaranty Trust, while opining that a cessation of lending would set back needed social change, did not deny that his bank was observing a moratorium on loans and that the future economic viability of South Africa was "a big question . . . "[157]

Another big question is how much actual lending to borrowers in South Africa is still going on, and whether it is possible to make a clear distinction between public and private, helpful and harmful loans in the South African context. Research is complicated by the fact that the South African government has made private placements of bond issues, and not all loans to private-sector borrowers are announced. Of the total $2.2 billion U.S. bank claims against South Africa, $47 million was placements with other banks and $1.186 billion was loans to public sector borrowers, leaving $968 million to private, nonbank borrowers.[158] Despite refinements of policy and finely-worded explanations to stockholders, the South African state and its economy are such that lending of any kind makes the banks, as much as the firms operating in South Africa, participants in the apartheid system.

The Political Impact of U.S. Investment in South Africa

Beyond their strategic role in the economy, American corporations in South Africa provide a crucial contribution to apartheid. U.S. investment and trade in South Africa create a material bond between U.S. corporations and the status quo regime. This bond, created by profits, provides the minority regime protection from meaningful economic sanctions. While economic sanctions are applied to socialist nations which the U.S. government opposes, they are not applied to a minority regime universally condemned for its violations of human rights. Clearly, U.S. corporations operating in South Africa would suffer economic hardships if sanctions were imposed. Thus, a U.S. administration which imposes restrictions on investment or trade is subject to intense pressure from corporate interests. Indeed, economic sanctions are considered "an extreme measure" by former Under Secretary of State for Political Affairs, Philip Habib.[159] When Henry Kissinger contemplated distancing the U.S. from Rhodesia by repealing the Byrd Amendment, he feared that multinational firms would end their support for the Ford administration. The Byrd Amendment, which allowed importation of Rhodesian chrome contrary to U.N. sanctions, was defended most strongly by Union Carbide and Allegheny-Ludlum, both heavily involved in importing chrome.[160]

According to Barbara Rogers, a former consultant to the chairperson of the House Subcommittee on Africa:

> American companies coordinate their activities on behalf of South Africa not only among themselves, but also with South African business interests, whether directly or through such bodies as the South Africa Foundation and United States South Africa Leadership Exchange Program, and of course with various agencies of the South African government.[161]

Their lobbying efforts are usually directed toward the Commerce and Treasury Departments, as opposed to the State Department, with Commerce frequently acting as an advocate of the companies' interests in interagency discussions of South African investment and trade policy.[162] Several directors of American firms with subsidiaries in South Africa have served at the highest levels of government. Among these are Kenneth Rush, president of Union Carbide from 1966-69 and then Deputy Secretary of Defense (1972-73) and Deputy Secretary of State (1973-74), and current Secretary of State Cyrus Vance, formerly a director of IBM.[163]

Besides support for maintaining existing relations, corporations can be a force encouraging closer ties with South Africa's minority regime. For example, Fluor Corporation led an unsuccessful effort in 1976 to repeal the ban on Export-Import Bank direct loans to South Africa. In the fall of 1977, 400 top American business executives, representing 325 major U.S. corporations, attended a seminar in New York to discuss why America should invest in South Africa. Former Secretary of the Treasury William E. Simon gave the keynote address:

> The United States is currently involved in a wide-ranging reassessment of its relations with South Africa. In my view that reassessment should lead to greater, not lesser, involvement with South Africa.[164]

U.S. mining companies, which often participate in joint ventures with

South African mining finance houses, use connections of key board members to convince U.S. government officials to strengthen American dependence on South Africa for strategic minerals. In turn, the National Commission on Materials Policy, citing South Africa as one of the few countries where U.S. firms could expect to mine strategic minerals, has recommended securing investments abroad against possible expropriation.[165]

Thus, as South African economist W.F.J. Steenkemp commented, "We (white South Africans) have learnt that our large economic relations are our best shield in a world which has chosen us as scapegoats."[166] In general, South Africa benefits from commercial relations by being included in the western political community. As was observed in the South African *Financial Gazette:*

> Through trade, South Africa can offer formidable resistance to any efforts to isolate her from the rest of the world. Foreign trade is in fact the means of ensuring a continued role for South Africa in world politics. Its political importance should, therefore, never be underestimated.[167]

South African whites will continue to depend on these economic relations as insurance against abandonment by the Western world.

U.S. Opposition to Apartheid: A Shield to Protect Investment and Prevent Radical Change

Profitable investment and trade is dependent upon a stable economic and political environment. When that environment is disturbed by radical change which questions basic assumptions about how goods and services are produced and distributed in a society, the capacity to create profits from investments and trade is greatly reduced. This simple relationship is a basic motivation of U.S. policy makers desiring pro-capitalist regimes throughout the world.

White South Africa, with its cheap labor, abundant resources, and strong anti-communist tone, provides a highly favorable economic climate. However, their racial policies trail western standards by a century on a continent where black people have been expelling colonial and racist regimes for the past 25 years. Pressure from black African nations has been a key motivation behind U.S. government condemnations of apartheid since the early 1960's. Yet concern about alienating black governments is rooted more in fear of losing profitable investments than in an honest concern for the aspirations of African peoples. Revolutionary struggle for independence, either armed or non-violent, has been perceived as a destabilizing factor serving the interests of communist nations.

Political Support for Investment

Only in tactics have U.S. corporate and government political goals in South Africa changed during the past 20 years. Basic concerns are twofold: to distance U.S. political connections to the obviously immoral minority regime in South Africa and to expand commercial ties. As has been made clear by ambassadors from Adlai Stevenson to Andrew Young, profitable economic relations are preferred to majority rule. In maintaining access to South Africa's profitable system of labor exploitation, different presidents have chosen different policies, damaging relations with black African nations to varying degrees. Thus, the major political objective of U.S. policy has been to encourage commercial activity without excessively harming America's image.

Although officially "the U.S. government neither encourages nor discourages investments in South Africa," it provides assistance to investors and exporters through a variety of government agencies. The U.S. Mission, according to former Assistant Secretary of State for African Affairs Nathaniel Davis, briefs U.S. businessmen on political, economic and social factors, reports significant economic developments, identifies major South African projects which have significant export potential, and assists U.S. businessmen in making appointments with potential South African customers.[168] A Department of Commerce study geared to potential investors in South Africa indicates:

> The U.S. Mission in South Africa, and particularly the economic and commercial officers consider the rendering of assistance to present and potential U.S. investors to be a vital part of its task in the country, and indeed, this commands a considerable portion of the officer's attention.[169]

Besides the work performed for investors and exporters by the Commerce Department and the U.S. Mission, the U.S. government facilitates economic interchange in a number of other ways, including direct government-financed credit, tax deductions, Export-Import Bank assistance, and the U.S. share of International Monetary Fund credit to South Africa. Direct credit covering the purchase of U.S. agricultural products to South African firms is extended by the Commodity Credit Corporation administered by the Department of Agriculture. From 1971 through 1977 this amounted to $60.4 million.[170]

Despite a ban on direct loans to South Africa since 1964, Export-Import Bank authorizations for South Africa have significantly increased in the 1970's. Compared to $42.8 million in 1971, loan guarantees and insurance totalled $205.4 million in 1976, with an additional $49 million in the transitional quarter, July 1-September 30, 1976. These figures exclude the discount loans for South Africa.[171] Relative to the size of their imports from the U.S., only three countries got more Ex-Im support in 1976 than South Africa, which received twice the world-wide average. An indication of the importance of such assistance came from the *Financial Mail*. Acknowledging that a good deal of foreign cash invested in South Africa consists of credits provided by overseas banks, partly underwritten by governmental export credit agencies like the Eximbank, the magazine went on to say:

> If these government guarantees were withdrawn, foreign banks would themselves have to bear the risk. In that event, they might choose not to grant the credits at all. The consequences could be a further drain on South Africa's reserves . . . [172]

Senator Dick Clark, chairman of the Senate Subcommittee on African Affairs, has recommended ending Ex-Im credit, which has helped South Africa obtain a range of commodities and technology crucial to infrastructure development and self-sufficiency.[173] After Committee hearings and compromises (mention of majority rule was struck), the House of Representatives voted to stop Ex-Im financing to the South African government, and its parastatal corporations, until the President determines that significant progress toward the elimination of apartheid has been made. Short of a complete cut-off of all Ex-Im funds, the amendment to the Bank's authorization bill requires that South African purchasers endorse and move toward implementation of certain fair employment practices before they are eligible for Ex-Im credit.[174]

Foreign tax credits, which allow corporations to deduct from U.S. taxes all taxes paid to a foreign nation, are also allowed in South Africa and Namibia. Allowing U.S. tax credits in Namibia blatantly supports South Africa's claim of sovereignty there, although the United Nations does not recognize the minority regime's authority. All corporate taxes for U.S. firms based in Namibia are paid directly to the white regime in South Africa and are deductable from U.S. taxes. A State Department official explains:

> The tax credit issue was carefully reviewed at the time the Treasury Department made its determination in 1973 that current U.S. law provides for a credit in the event of any payment of taxes on income to a governing power without regard to the legality of that government. Therefore, we do not consider that the granting of tax credits implies any recognition by the U.S. government of the legality of South Africa's taxing powers.[175]

In addition to maintaining commercial, defense, and agricultural attaches in South Africa, the U.S. government has cooperative agreements with the South African regime covering military/space tracking stations, nuclear technology, and other scientific advances including mining. Most interesting is the current policy of selling the white regime weapons-grade enriched uranium and sharing nuclear technology. A cooperative agreement permitting the export of nuclear technology and fuel has been in force since 1957. With U.S. corporate and government cooperation, South Africa's first nuclear reactor was inaugurated at Pelindaba near Pretoria in mid-1965, and the U.S. government has supplied enriched uranium to the South African regime ever since. Many of the nuclear technicians were trained at Oak Ridge, Tennessee and the main contractor for the project was Allis-Chalmers with eight other American firms involved.[176]

Historical Perspective

Although historically it has been assumed that America had no interests in Africa, American corporations have long maintained important investments on the continent, especially in resource rich southern Africa. According to Immanuel Wallerstein:

> " . . . up to 1960, the United States felt, correctly, that its interests were by and large, well protected by the tactical decisions of the four colonial powers Britain, France, Belgium and Portugal) plus South Africa."[177]

The lack of direct intervention in African affairs only indicates how successful colonial powers were at maintaining a favorable status quo. Inevitably, this dependence upon colonial policies placed the U.S. in opposition to Africans demanding their independence. In the 1950-s, men such as Dean Acheson and John Foster Dulles feared "premature" independence would lead to political instability resulting in Soviet domination of emerging African states. Yet when the transition to independence was moderate and peaceful, as in Kenya, America appeared to be a bystander and was easily able to adapt to the new status quo. Until the 1960's, with the exception of France's war in Algeria, western colonial powers were usually able to transfer political control to western oriented African elites who took the responsibility for insuring that trade and investment links with the free world would remain stable.

The interests of American policy makers in slowing change is clearly recorded in U.N. voting behavior during this period. In 1952, when South African apartheid first became an item on the U.N. agenda, the U.S. opposed the formation of the "Commission of the Racial Situation in Southern Africa." Not until 1958 had the Eisenhower Administration revised its position enough to vote for a resolution expressing "regret and concern" over South Africa's human rights violations. Yet even then the U.S. would not allow the word "condemn" to appear in the resolution.[178]

The Sharpeville Massacre and an American presidential election created a rhetorical break with former policy. On March 22, 1960, the State Department issued a statement voicing regret at "the tragic loss of life resulting from the measures taken against demonstrators."[179] This statement and John Kennedy's election established a new pattern in which the U.S. government joined a majority of U.N. delegates in verbal condemnation of South Africa. U.S. officials stopped short of endorsing any economic or military sanctions which implied that force was justified in bringing about change in the white regime's policy. In explaining why Kennedy did not support sanctions in 1962, Arthur Schlesinger, Jr. asserted that they were "at once grandiose and ineffectual."[180] Kennedy felt that as long as South Africa's major trading partners declined to participate, the call for an economic boycott would be meaningless.

Black African nations were not convinced by this rhetoric. At the first meeting of the Organization of African Unity in 1963, black leaders called on the U.S. to choose between Africa and the colonial powers. Schlesinger recalls: "After the (OAU) meeting, friendly African leaders like Houphouet-Boigny and Nyerere warned us that in the case of South Africa we could no longer rest on purely verbal condemnation of Apartheid."[181] Schlesinger implied this pressure motivated a policy discussion focused on how to satisfy African nationalists without endangering American interests.

Although State Department officials feared that instituting an arms embargo would only encourage African nationalists to ask for more stringent sanctions, Adlai Stevenson announced an embargo against arms shipments to South Africa in August 1963. A few days later he also supported a U.N. resolution to that effect. By announcing the embargo before U.N. action, he allowed continuing shipments of arms already sold and provided a mechanism for relaxing the embargo if the need arose in the future.[182] In summng up the policy debate over military sanctions, Schlesinger observed, "This action could not long satisfy the insatiable African demand for stronger measures against apartheid; but it preserved the new African faith in American policy."[183] The Kennedy administration's decision to support the embargo demonstrated the U.S. goal of defusing racial tensions via public relations.

Lyndon Johnson's administration continued Kennedy's policy of substituting rhetoric for action, but had little time to devote to Africa during the Vietnam war era. The Congo crisis was an exception. In 1964, American transport planes flew Belgian paratroopers to join South African mercenaries in crushing the Congolese nationalist forces to prevent the Soviet Union from gaining influence in southern Africa. As Steven Talbot observed:

The United States in effect replaced Belgium—which was too weak to handle the job—as the Western overseer of Zaire (the Congo), actively promoting the career of Colonel Joseph Mobutu, who took power in a 1965 military coup and has ruled the country ever since. Under Mobutu, Zaire became a haven for American investors, as well as one of Washington's main political allies in black-ruled Africa.[184]

With Richard Nixon's election, political restrictions on South Africa and Rhodesia were relaxed and investment rose dramatically. Between 1968 and 1973 American investment in South Africa increased 73% to $1.2 billion. Financed by corporations like Union Carbide (a major investor in southern Africa), Nixon's political coalition was less dependent on liberal and black support than Kennedy's and Johnson's.

Nixon's policy toward Africa was shaped, like all his foreign policy, by Henry Kissinger. During the years prior to 1974, when the Portuguese military revolution overthrew Caetano's colonial regime, Kissinger assumed: 1) white minority regimes in southern African were "here to stay;"[185] 2) blacks could not gain their goals through violence; and 3) "if violence in the area escalates, U.S. interests will increasingly be threatened."[186] From these premises, it seemed logical to discount support for black demands and favor closer ties and expanding commerce with white regimes.

These assertions are contained within Option 2 of the famous National Security Study Memorandum 39. This document, produced under the guidance of Kissinger by representatives of the CIA, and Departments of State and Defense, presents a comprehensive review of U.S. policy toward southern Africa "unadorned by rhetoric and devoid of charisma."[187]

Option 2 outlines a program designed to exert influence on blacks and whites to produce peaceful change "at an acceptable political cost."[188] The U.S. government should convince blacks "there is no hope . . .to gain the political rights they seek through violence, which will only lead to chaos and increased opportunities for the communists."[189] To encourage white regimes to change, the U.S. government "would indicate our willingness to accept political arrangements short of guaranteed progress toward majority rule, provided that they assure broadened political participation in some form by the whole population."[190]

Operational policy changes suggested by Option 2 include: liberalizing the arms embargo, removing constraints on Export-Import Bank facilities, "actively encouraging U.S. exports and facilitating U.S. investment," establishing flexible aid programs with black states, gradually relaxing sanctions on Rhodesia, and publicly opposing African "insurgent movements."[191]

Major advantages of adopting this program were twofold: first, it "would expand opportunities for profitable trade and investment," and second, by giving increased aid to black states it would "give them a tangible stake in accepting the prospects of gradual change."[192] The acceptable political risks Nixon administration officials were willing to take included greater criticism of U.S. policy and strained relations with black nations including Zambia and Tanzania.

NSSM 39 and its objectives were kept a closely guarded secret at the time. Although the Nixon and Ford administrations denied following Option 2, in retrospect one can see their decisions did converge with its stated goals. For example, helicopters and executive jet aircraft, easily convertible to security use, were licensed for sale to the South African government.[193] Other defense-related equipment was exported, including spare parts for C-130 transport planes, four IBM computers to the South African Defence Department, and two Foxboro Company computers, now being used to run a secret uranium enrichment plant outside Pretoria.[194] In 1972, the Nixon administration authorized the Eximbank to guarantee a ten-year loan to finance the sale of G.E. locomotives, thus overturing a former restriction on Ex-Im South Africa loans to five-year terms.[195] Despite strong State Department dissent, Union Carbide was allowed to import 115,000 tons of chrome ore from Rhodesia in 1970. The same request had been denied the previous two years.[196] Two years later, the Treasury Department chose to issue import licenses under the Byrd Amendment "not only for chrome ore but a number of other Rhodesian minerals as well."[197] In fact, the Byrd Amendment never encountered more than nominal opposition from the Nixon White House.

In 1972, the U.S. voted negatively at the United Nations on seven of the eight major issues related to southern Africa and colonialism. The U.S. was joined by South Africa and Portugal on these votes.[198] Perhaps the most penetrating indication of change in U.S. policy came from Donald McHenry, who now serves as Deputy Representative to the U.N., in testimony before the Senate Subcommittee on African Affairs:

> More important than specific actions was the changed tone of U.S. relations and the signal transmitted to blacks and whites alike. South African officials were warmly received in the White House and at the Department of Defense, sometimes without the knowledge of, and usually over the objection of, the Department of State. The American Ambassador in South Africa entertained on a discriminatory basis and, only after heavy criticism, was stopped by Washington from participating in opening of the Malan Theatre in Cape Town.[199]

With the Portuguese revolution and independence in Mozambique and Angola, politics in southern Africa were transformed. South Africa and Rhodesia now faced radical black governments on their borders. After the abortive intervention in Angola, which Kissinger seems to have undertaken to "prove he could stand up to the Russians,"[200] U.S. policy focused on non-military methods for preventing further erosion of western influence in the area.

On April 27, 1976, in Lusaka, Zambia, Secretary of State Henry Kissinger unveiled what he hoped would be interpreted as an entirely new U.S. policy toward southern Africa. He implied the U.S. would accept the principle of majority rule in Zimbabwe (Rhodesia) and Namibia (South West Africa). He also outlined a policy of extending broad new U.S. aid programs for the African continent and immediate assistance to promote development in southern Africa. By "acclerating economic development," Kissinger hoped he could insure moderate evolution toward majority rule.[201] In a press conference in September 1976, before his last mission in southern Africa, Kissinger stated:

> (Western countries) recognize the interests that they have in a moderate evolution of events in Africa . . . the consequences of the radicalization of Africa would be serious in many other parts of the world.[202]

To facilitate a peaceful solution, Kissinger's proposals at Lusaka included immediate programs of manpower training, rural development, advanced technology and modern transportation for both Zimbabwe and Namibia.[203] And in 1976 the Agency for International Development (AID) funded a massive study which mapped strategy for influencing the political outcomes in Namibia and Zimbabwe through foreign assistance programs. This study dealt with such questions as: "how to ensure the flow of foreign capital; how to ensure some stability in the administrative system; how to train an adequate number of African managers; how to prevent a necessary rise in African wages from disrupting the whole economy."[204] Although his Lusaka statement suspended previous emphasis upon relations with white states, Kissinger's new policy of intervening through foreign assistance was basically an extension of previous policies outlined in NSSM 39.

Jimmy Carter, who rode the tide of southern black support to victory, promised a new spirit in the White House. With regard to southern Africa, however, he has delivered no more than a "re-tread." He has publicly announced his support for continued investment in South Africa, and Ambassador Andrew Young has vetoed economic sanctions against South Africa in the U.N. Finally, reminiscent of the Kennedy years, Carter has taken steps to cultivate ties with black African nations to insure peaceful, pro-western governments throughout the continent and a moderate solution in Namibia and Zimbabwe.

An early item on Carter's agenda was the Zimbabwe crisis. In response to intense pressure from his black constituents and world opinion, the Carter administration undertook a campaign in Congress to repeal the Byrd Amendment. A review of both Andrew Young's and Cyrus Vance's testimony before Congress reveals that the Carter administration did not intend to diverge from Kissinger's major goal in southern Africa—protecting American economic interests from communist expansion by promoting peaceful change. As Andrew Young argued:

> We have also seen through the years increasingly militant government come upon the scene, to the extent that, I think, if we don't repeal the Byrd Amendment and move very rapidly toward majority rule in Zimbabwe, we will find ourselves facing chaos not only in Zimbabwe, but spilling over into Mozambique, Botswana, Zambia, and even into South Africa itself.[205]

The Carter administration fears militant, nationalist governments and socialist change in southern Africa because they may limit investment and trade opportunities available to U.S. business interests. As Cyrus Vance observed: "Intensified conflict in Rhodesia also entails serious adverse economic effects on countries in the region. Furthermore, the possibility of non-African forces interfering cannot be discounted."[206] In stressing the negative impact of revolutionary change in southern Africa, Carter administration officials deny that liberation movements have expressed the legitimate aspirations of black Africans from the FLA in Algeria to FRELIMO in Mozambique. This fear of outside forces determining southern Africa's fate, a polite reference to communism, confirms that U.S. government officials have not broken out of the cold war rhetorical categories which have long rationalized U.S. economic and political intervention to protect western capitalist economic interests abroad.

While his goals for Zimbabwe and Namibia do not differ from Kissinger's, Carter has enlisted black African support to obtain moderate western-oriented regimes in southern Africa. As Cyrus Vance stated before the NAACP convention in July of 1977:

> Our approach is to build positive relations with the Africans primarily through support for their political independence and economic development and through the strengthening of our economic, cultural and social ties.

Reminiscent of NSSM 29's goal of giving black states "a motive to co-operate in reducing tension," Vance continued:

> Our relations will be closest with those nations whose views and actions are most congruent with ours. We will never forget our take old friends for granted.[207]

Such policy statements have been accompanied by personal visits from Andrew Young and renewed offers of foreign assistance to co-operative African states.

One of the most outstanding examples of Washington's renewed interest in Africa has been the U.S.-Nigerian rapprochement, after years of estrangement under Kissinger's policies. Nigeria, Africa's most populous nation, now has the highest GNP on the continent and is the United States' second largest supplier of oil. At the August 1977, U.N.-sponsored conference for Action Against Apartheid held in Lagos and during Nigerian leader Lt. General Obasango' state visit to Washington the following October, the need to promote a moderate solution in southern Africa was emphasized. Nigeria supports and has given aid to the Patriotic Front of Zimbabwe.

Paradoxically, President Carter has repeatedly stated his opposition to apartheid, and at the same time, publicly announced his support for U.S. investment in South Africa. When asked by the *Financial Mail* if he would encourage investment in South Africa, Carter responded:

> Yes, indeed . . . economic development, investment commitment and the use of economic leverage against what is, after all, a government system of repression within South Africa, seems to me the only way to achieve racial justice there.[208]

Even next to the calculations of NSSM 39, the economic pressure Carter is talking about appears to be more an indication of his willingness to adopt economic intervention as a tactic for insuring continued western influence in the region than a viable way of achieving social justice.

By not ending the economic and political cooperation described earlier, the Carter administration's denunciation of apartheid goes no further than words. Export-Import Bank guarantees protect trade and South Africa's credibility. Tax credits encourage investment. U.S. contributions to the International Monetary Fund pay for South Africa's increased military spending.[209] Military and political attaches advise apartheid officials. And enriched uranium and shared nuclear technology give South Africa the potential to build nuclear weapons. The Congressional Black Caucus and other liberal Congresspeople have called upon the administration to end these supports and put a stop to new investment.[210]

Despite all these supports for American economic interests, Carter's rhetoric about majority rule has aroused criticism from corporate circles. In an influential article in the *Atlantic Monthly,* former Under Secretary of State George Ball asserted that by supporting a policy of one person, one vote, American policy was "fixed on an objective that depends in realistic terms on the blacks winning a civil war through the active intervention of a great power."[211] This statement, coming from a partner in Lehman Brothers Company and an elder statesman of the Democratic party, implies that Carter cannot take substantial steps toward ending apartheid without losing his business constituency.

Carter's unwillingness to impose sanctions on South Africa indicates the pressure being applied by the business community. During South Africa's recent crackdown on black opposition to apartheid, Andrew Young vetoed three U.N. resolutions proposing economic and military sanctions against South Africa. He did support a belated arms embargo, but, as the *Economist* observed, "the effect of this on South Africa's racial policy can be expected to be precisely nil."[212] In opposing sanctions, Young, reminiscent of Kennedy, asserted that they are not imposed to "make liberals feel good."[213] Historically, however, sanctions have been imposed by the U.S. government to destabilize radical governments from the Soviet Union, Cuba, and Chile to North Korea, Indonesia, and North Vietnam. Why not South Africa? Simply—it falls within the western oriented anti-communist status quo, and has a social system which produces large economic profits for U.S. corporations. As the Associated Press reported on October 27, 1977:

> From Chevrolets to copper to Coca Cola, American business is in South Africa in a big way—an economic fact of life that President Carter had to face in deciding what sanctions to support against the African nation's white-minority government.[214]

III.
The Withdrawal of U.S. Investment from South Africa

Just as American banks and corporations have helped to build and maintain apartheid through investing in South Africa, their disengagement can now assist in ending that system. Blacks within South Africa, representing a broad political spectrum, have called for this action. In doing so they cite two facts, both verified in the preceding sections.

First, the changing positions of blacks in the labor force, even if demanded by economic growth, will not bring down the apartheid system. By liberalizing their employment practices, U.S. firms cannot produce basic social change in South Africa.

Second, white wealth and power are significantly bolstered by American investment. Through their loans and business operations, U.S. companies contribute to a white-controlled economic surplus, make the internal security and military forces more effective, and help develop South Africa's strategic self-sufficiency.

The South African government knows foreign investment is vital to its continued survival and has worked hard to guarantee an ample flow. Among other policies, this has meant punishing domestic critics of foreign investment. Advocates of withdrawal can be charged under the Terrorism Act with crimes punishable by a minimum of five years imprisonment, and a maximum sentence of death. In 1975, nine members of the South African Student Organization (SASO) were charged with this crime and convicted. The charge sheet for one of these defendants read:

> In the Supreme Court of South Africa . . . The Attorney General of the Province of Transvaal, who as such prosecutes . . . on behalf of the State, presents and informs the Court that: . . . WHEREAS one Sipho Buthelezi . . . a member of the Executive Committee of . . . the Black People's Convention . . . did, upon the 31st of January 1973 . . . wrongfully, lawfully, and with intent to endanger the maintenance of law and order in the Republic or any portion thereof, write or cause to be written letters to . . . the companies . . . mentioned in Schedule "B" attached hereto, and thereby did . . . discourage, hamper, deter and/or prevent foreign investment in the

74

economy of the Republic . . . NOW therefore accused number (1) is guilty of the offense of participation in terroristic activities.[1]

The SASO nine received jail terms of five to ten years.

Despite such repression, black voices demanding economic sanctions continue to multiply and express the dominant view among black South Africans. The Christian Institute, banned in October 1977 as a result of its honesty in describing South African events, reported in 1976:

> Many black organizations have opposed foreign investment in South Africa, and this would be the opinion of the majority of South African blacks if their voices could be heard.[2]

This assessment is confirmed in a July 1977 report to Congress by Senator Dick Clark, chairman of the Subcommittee on African Affairs and head of a fact-finding mission to South Africa in late 1976. Senator Clark wrote:

> On my first visit to South Africa, most of those wanting change urged that the West should provide models of fair employment practices in their investments in South Africa. Now most favor more drastic economic action by the West—implying that new investment should be stopped, trade restrictions of some kind imposed, and perhaps even investment withdrawn, although to specifically advocate such measures is a crime.[3]

Major American newspapers have described the growing movement against American investments under headlines like "Black Opposition Mounts to U.S. Investment in S. Africa."[4] *The Washington Post* devoted an entire article in late 1977 to describing the disappointment among Soweto residents over America's failure to support economic sanctions in U.N. votes.[5]

Those now campaigning for an end to U.S. and other foreign investments in South Africa reflect the entire range of that country's black political activism, from liberation movements to black consciousness groups to a Bantustan official. The African National Congress and the Pan Africanist Congress, large movements suppressed in the early 1960's and now operating underground, have both long supported withdrawal of investment. The ANC argues:

> It is our firmly considered view that liberal opinion—however well intentioned it may appear—that opposes our campaign for this withdrawal is, in the long run, only delaying the change that is essential if South Africa is to be rid of apartheid and slave labor. It is not enough to grant higher wages here, better conditions there, for this leaves the apartheid system intact, in fact it props it up for longer—the very source of our misery and degradation.[6]

Newer organizatoins like SASO, the now-banned national black students organization, and the Black People's Convention (also recently banned), the leading cultural-political force among urban blacks in recent years, have made their position on foreign investment equally clear. A 1972 policy statement says that:

> SASO sees foreign investments as giving stability to South Africa's exploitative regime and committing South Africa's trading partners to supporting this regime. For this reason, SASO rejects foreign investments.
>
> Further, SASO sees the ameliorative experiences like those of Polaroid as at worst, conscience salving and at best, resulting in the creation of a change-resistant middle class amongst the few blacks employed by foreign firms.[7]

At their congress in December 1972, the Black People's Convention resolved, "To call upon foreign investors to disengage themselves from this white-controlled exploitative system."[8] Steve Biko founded SASO and was honorary president of the BPC. A considerably more conservative but equally well-known individual, Zulu Chief Gatsha Buthelezi, has come out in favor of economic sanctions, arguing that "sanctions are better than bloodshed," and he concluded:

> I honestly believe that the only way to salvage what is left of a chance for peaceful change is through the international community applying sanctions."[9]

Coloured and Indian organizations in South Africa have joined with Africans in supporting economic boycott of the country by foreign capital. At a 1972 convention of the South African Indian Congress, attended by 10,000, a resolution was passed "calling on foreign investors to withdraw their investments and operations from South Africa."[10] The executive body of the Coloured Labor Party, South Africa's largest Coloured political group, "has officially denounced foreign investments as detrimental to the oppressed in South Africa."[11] When Sonny Leon, head of the Party, attempted to travel outside South Africa to lecture against foreign investment, the government denied him authorization to leave.

In the face of demands that they end their involvement in South Africa, American corporations typically charge that those calling for withdrawal are misguided. If we get out, they argue, blacks will suffer most, as a result of lost jobs and income and heightened government repression.

It is true that any economic sanctions against South Africa will produce black unemployment as well as white. And it is likely that the government's initial reaction to such foreign pressure will be another series of crackdowns. No black South African calls for withdrawal without considering these realities. It is they and their constituents, relatives and friends who will be affected. Nevertheless, they see these short-term costs as a prerequisite for their freedom, just as the hundreds who died in township uprisings during the summer of 1976 did. As the late Chief Albert Luthuli, Nobel Peace Prize winner and one-time President of the ANC, said:

> The economic boycott of South Africa will entail undoubted hardship for Africans. We do not doubt that. But if it is a method which will shorten the day of blood, the suffering to us will be a price we are willing to pay. In any case, we suffer already, our children are often undernourished, and, on a small scale (so far), we die at the whim of a policeman.[12]

Chief Luthuli's words are echoed in those of individual black South Africans reacting to the Security Council's failure to impose economic sanctions following the October 1977 wave of bannings.

> What Joel Makwele read last week did not please him. At the United Nations, an arms embargo against South Africa was approved, but not the credit and investment sanctions that might force Pretoria to rethink its apartheid policies. Mr. Makwele, a "helper" to a white mechanic at a United States-owned company in Johannesburg, might lose his job if the full range of sanctions was approved. But he still wanted an economic boycott that would force whites to choose between racial privilege and prisperity.[13]
>
> (an industrial worker)

> I am disappointed. The trade and commercial enterprises are the topmost priority. They should have been first priority—cut off completely—because, as they say, we blacks have got nothing to lose.[14]
>
> (a community leader)

> The better for the Carter Administration to pull out now. We have suffered for 300 years now, and if that means we have to suffer for two or three more decades even, it won't matter.[15]
>
> (a Soweto businessman)

> Forty per cent of my goods are American. Take them away and who do you hurt? The African? We can live on mush and water.[16]
>
> (a Soweto shopkeeper)

These South Africans regard their hardships under the status quo to to be so real that sanctions cannot make them qualitatively worse. This is not difficult to understand, given that black unemployment now stands at 25%; wages for those who do have work are at the poverty line; and a record number of blacks are currently under political detention. They believe that just as whites benefit disproportionately from the health of the economy, so can whites be made to feel the brunt of its stagnation under sanctions. American business leaders can persist in their self-serving argument that sanctions will hurt more than help, but it is clear that most South African blacks do not share their belief.

Confirmation that this is the case recently surfaced from a surprising source—the American Embassy in Pretoria. In March 1977 Ambassador Bowdler cabled a confidential report to the State Department that said:

> Among Black youth and more militant groups, as well as some businessmen, any foreign investment is viewed as propping up the South African economy and its social system. They argue that jobs provided are marginal compared to numbers suffered from apartheid.

Taking all points of view into account, the Ambassador was forced to conclude that the

> role of American firms (in South Africa) will become increasingly controversial and rationale for continued presence will seem less and less persuasive to growing numbers of blacks.[17]

White South Africa greatly fears the impact of economic sanctions, including the withdrawal of investment. This can be seen in the current "get tough" attitude; in the public relations seminars designed to reassure U.S. investors; in the large promotional inserts on South Africa appearing in Western financial journals like *Business Week*; in numerous articles on the impact of sanctions dotting the pages of the Johannesburg *Star* and other newspapers; in the tightening of regulations covering the repatriation of foreign capital; in the Minister of Economic Affairs' November 1977 activation of the National Supplies Procurement Act, under which any company operating in South Africa can be forced to manufacture and deliver goods determined essential to national security; and in the government's juggernaut drive for industrial self-sufficiency.

The white fear of Western economic disengagement has been well articulated by the director of the South African Institute of International Affairs:

> Any country in the modern world needs working relations with other countries. It needs contacts for trade, capital, technological know-how, scientific and cultural exchange: all the things which keep a country alive in the modern world. If a society is cut off, the danger is that it will simply wither.[18]

It has been estimated that a total new investment boycott in 1976 alone would have lowered gross domestic production by up to 5% and created as much as 40,000 additional unemployed whites and 80,000 more unemployed non-whites.[19] This would have been a 400% boost in white unemployment in an economy where whites wihtout work are virtually unheard of, and an approximate 5% increase in non-white unemployment in a black labor force which already has over 1,500,000 jobless.[20] Moreover, the material impact of economic sanctions will not be so much in the first year or two of their imposition, but over the course of five to seven years when the cost structure of South African industry will rise, unemployment skyrocket and inefficiencies abound.[21]

At the moment, South Africa's economy is particularly vulnerable. Since the 1973 Arab oil embargo, it has been in the doldrums. World inflation spurred by oil price hikes have hit the economy hard. South Africa now suffers from chronic double digit inflation. Recession in America and Western Europe has depressed her export markets. And the government is demanding increasing revenue for military expenditures and strategic public works projects. These financial realities, combined with political uncertainty, have produced reticence among foreign investors. Between January and June of 1977, South Africa experienced a net outflow of R649 million in foreign capital.[22] Commenting on the country's critical need for foreign investment in light of these events, the *Financial Mail* stated:

> So long as we have to repay foreign capital we have to export more than we import, and save more than we invest. That means still lower living standards . . . government's proper priority should be to restore local and foreign confidence . . . it will have to come up with some genuine political answers.[23]

The political answer the government came up with after the Sharpeville massacre was greater repression of the black population, and the West responded with renewed massive investment. To prevent a repetition of this scenario, economic and political pressure from groups within the investor countries is necessary.

Such pressure has been building in the United States. In addition to university students on over 100 campuses who have organized to demand that their schools sell all stocks and bonds in corporations that invest in South Africa, a growing number of labor unions, churches, civil rights organizations, and human rights groups have taken a stand against apartheid. In cities across the country there are ongoing campaigns to end financial support by getting individuals and institutions to withdraw their accounts from banks that lend to South Africa. The National Council of Churches called on its 30 constituent denominations to "undertake" to remove funds from banks that deal wtih the South African government or businesses and the NAACP has come out for total withdrawal of American companies. In February 1978 the AFL-CIO Executive Council declared that "U.S. corporations should immediately divest themselves of South African affiliates, and sever all ties with South African corporations." Union pension funds, such as the United Automobile Workers' (UAW) and the National Hospital and Health Care Workers' (District 1199), and state retirement systems from Connecticut to California are examining their portfolios, closing their accounts with accomplice banks, and banning investment in South Africa. Public officials and state legislatures have begun to express concern and take action—Madison, Wisconsin will give preference in bids to firms that do no business in South

Africa; the Gary, Indiana city council has limited its purchases from companies that sell there; and the state of Michigan adopted a resolution calling for Congress and the President to impose sanctions against the South African government. Illustrative of a range of activity and variety of tactics, these examples show that a national anti-apartheid movement has begun.[24]

Disengagement

An American firm can disengage itself from South Africa through a number of mechanisms. The most politically effective of these is probably a rapid scaling down of operations. This means halting the flow of new money, technology and personnel to the South African subsidiary while at the same time increasing the proportion of earnings remitted to the parent company overseas.[25] Since fixed investments constantly depreciate, this will have the effect of using up the capital incorporated in the subsidiary. All the company will leave behind are some outdated, deteriorating physical assets. The analogous option for banks is the halting of all new loans to South Africa and a refusal to renew old ones.

The other mechanisms of disengagement all involve selling the subsidiary to other South African or foreign interests. Under South African exchange control laws, the proceeds of such a sale must be converted securities rands. These securities rands can then be repatriated in one of four ways.[26] First, a U.S. company can purchase non-residential bonds issued by the South African Treasury. These bonds mature after five years and can then be redeemed for proceeds remittable abroad. Second, a company can purchase certain government, municipal and public utility bonds and national savings certificates. After being held for five years these may be cashed in for currency remittable abroad. Third, a firm can purchase stocks quoted locally on the Johannesburg Stock Exchange. These stocks can be exported immediately and sold freely on a foreign stock exchange for dollars. Fourth, a corporation can sell its securities rand to another foreign investor for dollars. While the South African government has made it difficult for a foreign investor to remit the proceeds from the sale of a subsidiary, it has not made it impossible. All of these exchange control regulations can cushion the short-term impact of a substantial flight of capital, but they cannot shield the economy from the ultimate effect of being denied access to multinational investment, bank loans, expertise, imports, and export markets.

Disengagement may not be the decisive pressure for majority rule, but it can act as a catalyst for other forces. More than one-half of black South Africa is under the age of 25. This group is making it increasingly clear that it does not want to take its place among past generations which have been born, lived and died under the bootheel of white rule.

No authoritarian ruling party has ever forfeited power as long as it was confident it could continue to triumph through force. U.S. corporate involvement in South Africa strengthens the status quo and encourages complacency among whites regarding fundamental political change. The withdrawal of American firms would weaken this status quo and create hope among black South Africans that they can effectively challenge the regime. "Business as usual" means "apartheid as usual." As an American source at the U.N. put it, "there is ample evidence that our policy of sweet reasonableness has not worked."

References

Section One

1. For progressive force arguments see: William Hance, "The Case For and Against U.S. Disengagement From South Africa," in Hance, ed., *Southern Africa and the United States* (New York, Columbia University Press, 1968); M.O. Dowd, "The Stages of Economic Growth and the Future of South Africa," cited in Report of the SPROCAS Political Commission, *South Africa's Political Alternatives* (Johannesburg, SPROCAS, 1973); Corporate Information Center Brief, "The Withdrawal Debate," *Corporate Examiner,* June, 1973; Martin Legassick, "Foreign Investment and the Reproduction of Racial Capitalism," unpublished; and various corporate proxy statements and annual reports.

2. *Financial Mail,* September 11, 1970.

3. Legassick, op. cit., p. 1.

4. Donald McHenry, *United States Firms in South Africa,* Study Project on External Investment in South Africa and Namibia (Indiana University, 1975), appendix.

5. Our presentation of this evidence draws upon and parallels that of Martin Legassick, F.A. Johnstone, Simmons and Simmons, and Harold Wolpe.

6. UNESCO, *Racism and Apartheid in Southern Africa.*

7. Study Project on Christianity in Apartheid Society, Economics Commission, *Power, Privilege and Poverty* (Johannesburg, Christian Institute); and Martin Legassick, "South Africa: Forced Labour, Industrialization and Racial Discrimination," in Richard Harris, ed., *Political Economy of Africa* (Boston, Schenkman, 1974), p. 238.

8. Legassick, op. cit., p. 242.

9. F.A. Johnstone, *Class, Race and Gold: A Study of Class Relations and Racial Discrimination in South Africa* (London, 1973).

10. Legassick, op. cit., p. 245.

11. Ibid.

12. Harold Wolpe, "Capitalism and Cheap Labour Power in South Africa: From Segregation to Apartheid," *Economy and Society,* 1, 1972.

13. Ibid.

14. Martin Legassick, "South Africa: Capital Accumulation and Violence," *Economy and Society,* 3, 1974, p. 267.

15. SPROCAS, op. cit., pp. 50-55; Legassick, "Capital Accumulation and Violence," op. cit., pp. 265-266; Robert Davis, "Industrial Relations Legislation . . . , " *Review of African Political Economy,* Sept.-Dec., 1976.

16. SPROCAS, op. cit., pp. 34-36.

17. Harrison Wright, *The Burden of the Present* (Cape Town, D. Philip, 1977), p. 12.

18. Legassick, "South Africa: Forced Labour Industrialization and Racial Discrimination," op. cit.

19. Legassick, "Capital Accumulation and Violence," op. cit., p. 268.

20. Alex Callinicas and John Rogers, *Southern Africa After Soweto* (London, Pluto Press, 1977).

21. Ibid.

22. Alex Hepple, *South Africa: Workers Under Apartheid* (London, Christian Action, 1971).

23. Wolpe, op. cit.

24. Callinicas and Rogers, op. cit., p. 47.

25. Legassick, "Capital Accumulation and Violence," op. cit., p. 275.

26. Ibid., pp. 274-277.

27. Brian Bunting, "The Origins of Apartheid," in Alex La Guma, ed., *Apartheid* (London, Lawrence and Wishart Ltd., 1972), p. 25.

28. F.A. Johnstone, "White Prosperity and White Supremacy in South Africa Today," *African Affairs*, April 1970, pp. 124-140.

29. Bunting, op. cit., p. 28.

30. Ibid., pp. 28-29.

31. See discussion by Heribert Adam, *Modernizing Racial Discrimination* (Berkeley, Univ. of Calif. Press, 1971); and Johnstone, "White Prosperity . . .," op. cit.

32. U.N. Unit on Apartheid, *Industrialization, Foreign Capital and Forced Labour in South Africa* (United Nations, New York, 1970), p. 30.

33. Ibid., p. 31.

34. Ibid., pp. 31-32.

35. U.N. Unit on Apartheid, op. cit.

36. International Defence and Aid Fund, *Apartheid Quiz* (London, I.D.A.F., 1976), p. 17.

37. David Davis, *African Workers and Apartheid* (London, International Defense and Aid Fund, 1978), p. 5.

38. Ibid., p. 4.

39. Barbara Rogers, *Divide and Rule: South Africa's Bantustans* (London, International Defense and Aid Fund), p. 21.

40. Ibid., p. 20.

41. *Apartheid Quiz,* op. cit., p. 5.

42. Rogers, op. cit., p. 11.

43. Ibid., p. 10.

44. Ibid.

45. *Apartheid Quiz,* op. cit., p. 35.

46. Ibid., pp. 37-38.

47. See Amnesty International, United Nations, and other reports. See also conventional media coverage of Steve Biko's death—October-December, 1977.

48. U.N. Unit on Apartheid, op. cit., p. 27.

49. Ernest Harsch, "The Foreign Economic Role in South Africa," *Intercontinental Press,* April 18, 1977, p. 434.

50. William Duggan, *A Socioeconomic Profile of South Africa* (New York, Praeger, 1973), p. 66.

51. Harsch, op. cit., p. 391.

52. Duggan, op. cit., p. 65.

53. Ernest Harsch, "The U.S. Corporate Stake in South Africa," *Intercontinental Press,* April 18, 1977, p. 434.

54. Sandra Van Der Merwe, *The Environment of South African Business* (Cape Town, 1976), p. 107.

55. *X-Ray: Current Affairs in South Africa,* January-February, 1976, p. 1.

56. See Hance, op. cit., and IRRC, *Labor Practices of U.S. Corporations in South Africa,* Special Report 1976-A, April 1976, pp. 24-25.

57. Duggan, op. cit., p. 118.

58. IRRC, op. cit., p. 42.

59. Van Der Merwe, op. cit., p. 181.

60. South African Dept. of Information, *Official Yearbook of the Republic of South Africa: 1976* (Johannesburg, Perskor Printers, 1976), p. 503.

61. South African Institute of Race Relations, *A Survey of Race Relations in South Africa: 1974* (Johannesburg, Natal Witness, 1975), p. 257.

62. Van Der Merwe, op. cit., p. 185.

63. Ibid.

64. Information Counselor, South African Embassy, Washington, D.C., *Backgrounder,* No. 3, 1978. p. 3.

65. SPROCAS, op. cit., p. 90.

66. Ruth First, et. al., *The South African Connection* (Great Britain, Harper and Row, 1972), Ch. 4.

67. Ibid., p. 73.

68. *Annual Survey of Race Relations: 1976,* op. cit., p. 276.

69. Francis Wilson, "The Political Implications for Blacks of Economic Changes Now Taking Place in South Africa," in Leonard Thompson and Jeffrey Butler, *Change in Contemporary South Africa* (Univ. of Calif. Press, 1975), p. 182.

70. *Annual Survey of Race Relations: 1976,* op. cit., p. 262.

71. South African Dept. of Information, op. cit., p. 472.

72. Ibid.

73. Wilson, op. cit., p. 183.

74. Ibid., pp. 173, 1978.

75. Natrass, op. cit.

76. Mary Benson, *The Struggle for a Birthright* (London, Penguin Books, 1966), p. 49. E. Roux, *Time Longer Than Rope* (London, 1948) puts the figure at a quarter-million.

77. M. Horrell, *South Africa's Workers* (Johannesburg, South African Institute of Race Relations, 1969), p. 8.

78. David Davis, op. cit., pp. 31-32.

79. Ibid.

80. Ibid., p. 33.

81. Ibid., p. 32, based on information from International Defence and Aid Fund, *Workers Under Apartheid* (London, IDAF, 1971).

82. Testimony of Jerry Funk before the Senate Subcommittee on African Affairs, Sept. 22, 1976, p. 433.

83. Davis, op. cit., p. 25 and S.A. Institute of Race Relations, Annual Survey of Race Relations, 1974, pp. 325-326.

84. Davis, op. cit., p. 25.

85. Ibid., p. 27.

86. Testimony of Jerry Funk, op. cit., p. 430.

87. Davis, op. cit., p. 36.

88. Counter Information Services, *Black South Africa Explodes* (Washington, D.C., Transnational Institute, 1976).

89. Davis, op. cit., p. 29.

90. T.R.H. Davenport, *South Africa: A Modern History* (Toronto: Univ. of Toronto Press, 1977), p. 304.

91. *Annual Survey of Race Relations: 1976,* op. cit., p. 315.

92. Ibid., pp. 317-318.

93. South African Dept. of Information, op. cit., p. 478.

94. Ibid., pp. 477-478.

95. "One Factory, One Union," *Financial Mail,* July 15, 1977.

96. *South Africa-Namibia Update,* June 29, 1977, p. 3.

97. Giovanni Arrighi, "International Corporations, Labor Aristocracies, and Economic Development in Tropical Africa," in Arrighi and Saul, *Essays on the Political Economy of Africa* (New York, Monthly Review Press, 1973).

98. Heribert Adam, "Internal Constellations and Potentials for Change," in Thompson, op. cit., p. 324.

99. Stephen Talbot, "United States Intervention in Southern Africa: The New Era," *Socialist Revolution,* July-August, 1977.

100. *South African Digest,* June, 1977.

101. IRRC, op. cit., p. 29.

102. *San Francisco Chronicle,* Dec. 8, 1977.

103. Heribert Adam, "South African Power Elite," in Adam, *South Africa: Sociological Perspectives* (London, Oxford Univ. Press, 1971).

104. Talbot, op. cit., pp. 28-29.

105. *Southern Africa,* October 1977, p. 12.

106. Jim Hoagland, *South Africa: Civilization in Conflict* (New York: Houghton Mifflin, 1972), p. 64.

107. *Wall Street Journal,* March 16, 1977.

108. IRRC, op. cit., p. 84.

109. *Financial Mail,* March 4, 1977.

Section Two

1. Albie Sachs, "The Instruments of Domination in South Africa," in Thompson and Butler, ed., op. cit., p. 223.

2. South African Dept. of Information, *Official Yearbook of the Republic of South Africa* (Johannesburg, 1976), pp. 147-164.

3. South African Institute of Race Relations, *Annual Survey of Race Relations: 1976* (Johannesburg, Natal Witness, 1977), p. 207.

4. Sachs, op. cit.

5. Counter Information Services, op. cit.,

6. *Wall Street Journal,* December 3, 1976.

7. *Annual Survey of Race Relations: 1976,* p. 35.

8. *X-Ray: Current Events in Southern Africa,* "The Cost of Apartheid," March-April, 1977.

9. Ruth First, et. al., *The South African Connection* (Great Britain, Harper and Row, 1972).

10. Barbara Rogers, *White Wealth and Black Poverty: American Investments in Southern Africa* (Westport, Conn., Greenwood Press, 1976), p. 97.

11. Ibid., p. 96.

12. U.N. Unit on Apartheid, *Industrialization, Foreign Capital and Forced Labour in South Africa* (United Nations, New York, 1970), Ch. 4.

13. South African Federal Reserve Bank, *Quarterly Bulletin,* June 1977.

14. Investor Responsibility Research Center, *U.S. Business and South Africa: The Withdrawal Issue, Special Report 1977-D,* November 1977, p. 3.

15. John Burns, "Full Sanctions Awkward: South Africa is Big Business," *New York Times,* November 6, 1977.

16. U.N. Commission on Transnational Corporations, "Activities of Transnational Corporations in Southern Africa and the Extent of Their Collaboration With the Illegal Regimes in the Area," April 6, 1977.

17. Burns, op. cit.

18. Ernest Harsch, "The Foreign Economic Role in South Africa," *Intercontinental Press,* April 11, 1977, p. 393.

19. Rogrs, op. cit., pp. 100-101.

20. Colin Legum, *Vorster's Gamble For Africa,* p. 87.

21. U.N. Unit on Apartheid, op. cit., and C.P. de Kock, "South Africa's Balance of Payments," *South African Banker,* May 1977.

22. C.P. de Kock, op. cit.

23. *Financial Mail,* "Financing the Republics," July 2, 1976.

24. U.N. Unit on Apartheid, op. cit., p. 60.

25. John Suckling, et. al., *The Economic Factor* (London, Africa Publications Trust, 1975), p. 23.

26. *Science,* July 20, 1970, p. 159.

27. Tami Hultman and Reed Kramer, "South Africa's Growing Nuclear Prowess," *L.A. Times,* August 28, 1977, Part IV, p. 1.

28. J. Spence, *The Military and Political Framework* (London, African Publications Trust, 1975).

29. Burns, op. cit.

30. IRRC, Analysis E, No. 4, p. E-55.

31. U.N. Notes and Documents, No. 8/77, April 1977.

32. Ian Mackler, *Pattern for Profit in Southern Africa* (Lexington, Mass., D.C. Heath, 1972), p. 111.

33. U.N. Unit on Apartheid, op. cit., Ch. 4, and Rogers, op. cit., p. 125.

34. South African Dept. of Information, op. cit., pp. 491-510.

35. Ann and Neva Seidman, "American Multinationals in South Africa," *Journal of Southern African Affairs,* Special Issue/Oct. 1976, p. 133.

36. IRRC, *U.S. Business and South Africa,* op. cit., p. 5.

37. Rogers, op. cit., p. 141.

38. IRRC, *U.S. Business and South Africa,* op. cit., pp. 38 and 44.

39. IRRC, Analysis E, No. 9.

40. Interfaith Center on Corporate Responsibility, *The Expansion of Foreign Oil Companies in South Africa,* March 1976, p. 6.

41. Ibid.

42. Rogers, op. cit., p. 141.

43. Interfaith Center on Corporate Responsibility, op. cit.

44. IRRC, Analysis E, No. 9.

45. Interfaith Center on Corporate Responsibility, op. cit., p. 10.

46. IRRC, Analysis E, No. 9.

47. Ibid.

48. Testimony of Jennifer Davis, Research Director, African Fund, Senate Subcommittee on African Affairs, Sept. 29, 1976, p. 672.

49. Ibid.

50. Corporate Information Center Brief, "Mobil and Rhodesia," *The Corporate Examiner,* October, 1977.

51. ICCR, op. cit., pp. 12-13.

52. Ibid., p. 7.

53. *Financial Mail,* June 15, 1977.

54. IRRC, *U.S. Business and South Africa,* op. cit., pp. 38, 40, 41.

55. Rogers, op. cit., p. 128.

56. Testimony of A.A. Cunningham, V.P. General Motors, Senate Subcommittee on African Affairs, Sept. 22, 1976, p. 452.

57. Rogers, op. cit., p. 127.

58. Ibid.

59. Ralph Horwitz, *The Political Economy of South Africa* (London, Wendenfeld and Nicholson, 1967), p. 328.

60. Economic Priorities Report, "Chrysler, Ford and General Motors in South Africa," October-November 1970, Council on Economic Priorities, pp. 9-11.

61. Don Morton, *Partners in Apartheid,* Council for Christian Social Action, June, 1973, p. 23.

62. Economic Priorities Report, op. cit., p. 9.

63. Ibid., p. 24.

64. IRRC, Analysis E, No. 12, p. E-149.

65. Rogers, op. cit., pp. 129-130.

66. *Church Investments, Corporations and Southern Africa,* Corporate Information Center (New York, Friendship Press, 1973), p. 78.

67. *The New York Times,* May 18, 1978.

68. Rogers, op. cit., pp. 129-30.

69. Economic Priorities Report, op. cit., p. 12.

70. *The New York Times,* May 18, 1978. For text of memo, see *Souther Africa,* Volume XI, No. 5, June/July 1978.

71. "Computers: Where, What and When," *Management,* Novembe 1974, p. 33.

72. U.N. Commission on Transnational Corporations, op. cit., p. 23.

73. U.N. Commission on Transnational Corporations, op. cit., and *Churc Investments,* op. cit., p. 101.

74. *Management,* op. cit., p. 33.

75. Rogers, op. cit., p. 133.

76. Testimony of Gilbert Jones, Vice-Chairman, IBM, Senate Subcom mittee on African Affairs, Sept. 29, 1976, p. 652; and Larry Gordon, Repoi to District of Columbia City Government, unpublished, June, 1975, p. 10.

77. Rogers, op. cit., p. 135.

78. Testimony of Jennifer Davis, op. cit., p. 673.

79. *Management,* op. cit., Gordon, op. cit., and Testimony of Gilber Jones, op. cit.

80. Testimony of Gilbert Jones, op. cit.; quoting Chairman of the Board of IBM, p. 678.

81. Church Project on U.S. Investment in Southern Africa, Statement for IBM proxy solicitation, March 15, 1975, p. 3.

82. Testimony of Gilbert Jones, op. cit., p. 683.

83. Testimony of Jennifer Davis, op. cit., p. 674.

84. Gordon, op. cit., p. 3.

85. Ibid., p. 9.

86. Church Project on U.S. Investments . . . , op. cit., p. 3.

87. U.N. Commission on Transnational Corporations, op. cit., p. 26.

88. Ibid., p. 25.

89. Ernest Harsch, "The U.S. Corporate Stake in South Africa," *Inter-continental Press,* April 18, 1977, p. 434.

90. Duggan, op. cit., pp. 70-80.

91. South African Dept. of Information, op. cit., Ch. 22.

92. Ibid., p. 555.

93. *New York Times,* September 4, 1972.

94. Ann and Neva Seidman, op. cit., p. 144.

95. Harsch, op. cit., p. 433.

96. South African Dept. of Information, op. cit., p. 568.

97. Rogers, op. cit., p. 143.

98. IRRC, Special Report 1977-D, November, 1977, p. 45.

99. IRRC, Analysis E, No. 11, p. E-139.

100. *Los Angeles Times,* "Phelps Dodge, S. African Group Plans Mine Project," undated, 1977.

101. Rogers, op. cit., p. 144.

102. Corporate Information Center Brief, op. cit., pp. 3B-3C; and IRRC, Analysis E, No. 10.

103. Seidman, op. cit., p. 144.

104. IRRC, Analysis E, No. 3, p. E-47.

105. Ibid.

106. Van Der Merwe, op. cit., p. 23.

107. Interfaith Center on Corporate Responsibility, *General Electric in South Africa,* New York, 1977.

108. IRRC, Analysis E, No. 3, p. E-46.

109. Rogers, op. cit., p. 132.

110. IRRC, *U.S. Business and South Africa . . . ,* op. cit., p. 39; and *Church Investments,* op. cit., p. 146.

111. IRRC, Ibid., p. 38; and *Church Investments,* Ibid., p. 52.

112. *The South African Military-Industrial Complex and University Investments,* People for Southern African Freedom, U. of Oregon, 1977.

113. *Johannesburg Star,* November 27, 1977.

114. Testimony of Thomas Green, V.P. Norton Co., Senate Subcommittee on African Affairs, Sept. 22, 1976, p. 436.

115. U.N. Commission on Transnational Corporations, op. cit., p. 24.

116. IRRC, *U.S. Business and South Africa,* op. cit., p. 41.

117. IRRC, Analysis E, No. 2, p. E-33.

118. *Church Investments,* op. cit., pp. 61-62, and IRRC, *U.S. Business and South Africa,* op. cit., p. 40.

119. U.N. Commission on Transnational Corporations, op. cit., p. 24.

120. Gordon, op. cit., p. 23.

121. IRRC, *U.S. Business and South Africa,* op. cit., Appendix B.

122. Seidman, op. cit., p. 150.

123. Rogers, op. cit., p. 138.

124. *Church Investments,* op. cit., p. 155.

125. *South Africa Digest,* September 19, 1977.

126. *Church Investments,* op. cit., p. 164.

127. Tami Hultman and Reed Kramer, op. cit.

128. Seidman, op. cit., p. 153.

129. *Church Investments,* op. cit., p. 160.

130. Ibid., pp. 118-119.

131. IRRC, Analysis E, No. 4, p. E-55.

132. Ibid.

133. Committee to Stop Banking on Apartheid.

134. Corporate Information Center Brief, "Banking on Apartheid," *The Corporate Examiner,* October, 1976.

135. Reed Kramer, "In Hock to U.S. Banks," *The Nation,* December 11, 1976; and CIC Brief "Banking on Apartheid," op. cit.

136. IRRC, Analysis E, No. 4, p. E-55.

137. Heribert Adam, *Modernizing Racial Domination* (Berkeley, Univ. of Calif. Press, 1971), footnote, p. 29.

138. Rogers, op. cit., pp. 101-102.

139. *Washington Post,* January 16, 1977; Spence, op. cit., p. 55; and *Annual Survey of Race Relations: 1976,* p. 35.

140. IRRC, Analysis E, No. 4, p. E-54.

141. *Financial Mail,* July 2, 1976.

142. Ernest Harsch, "American Dollars to Pretoria's Rescue," *Intercontinental Bulletin,* May 2, 1977, p. 481.

143. CIC Brief, op. cit.

144. Ernest Harsch, "The Foreign Economic Role in South Africa," op. cit., p. 392.

145. CIC Brief, op. cit.

146. Ibid.

147. Ernest Harsch, "The Foreign Economic Role . . . ," op. cit., p. 392.

148. Ernest Harsch, "American Dollars . . . , " op. cit., p. 481.

149. *Financial Mail,* August 26, 1977, p. 775.

150. Ernest Harsch, "American Dollars . . . ," op. cit., p. 481.

151. Ernest Harsch, "The Foreign Economic Role . . . ," op. cit., p. 392.

152. *South African Digest,* October 15, 1976.

153. IRRC, Analysis E, No. 1.

154. *Financial Mail,* July 2, 1976.

155. Testimony of Timothy Smith, Director ICCR, Senate Subcommittee on African Affirs, op. cit., Sept. 23, 1976, p. 550.

156. *The New York Times,* March 11, 1978.

157. *The Washington Post,* April 13, 1978.

158. *American Banker,* March 14, 1978.

159. Hearings before the Subcommittee on Africa of the Committee on International Relations, House of Representatives, March 3, 1977.

160. Mark Bellamy, Pacific News Service, May 6, 1976.

161. Barbara Rogers, et. al., *The Great White Hoax* (London, Africa Bureau, 1977), p. 77.

162. Ibid.

163. Seidman, op. cit., p. 144.

164. Information Counselor, South African Embassy, Washington, D.C., Backgrounder, No. 8, 1977, p. 1.

165. Ann and Neva Seidman, *South Africa and U.S. Multinational Corporations* (Westport, Conn., Lawrence Hill, 1978), p. 84, 87-88.

166. Corporate Information Center Brief, "U.S. Corporate Expansion in S.A., *Corporate Examiner,* April, 1976, p. 3A.

167. Africa Research Group, *Race to Power* (New York, Anchor Press, 1974), p. 119.

168. Hearings before the Subcommittee on African Affairs of the Committee on Foreign Relations, United States Senate, July 24, 1975, p. 354.

169. Mackler, op. cit.

170. James Morrell, "U.S. Financial Aid to South Africa, 1971-1977," Center for International Policy, Washington, D.C., November 7, 1977, 1 page mimeo.

171. Ibid.

172. Testimony of Edgar Lockwood, Executive Director, Washington Office on Africa before the Subcommittee on International Trade of House Committee on Banking, February 9, 1978.

173. Senator Dick Clark, *U.S. Corporate Interests in South Africa,* Report to Senate Committee on Foreign Relations, January 1978.

174. House *Congressional Record,* June 2, 1978.

175. Senate Subcommittee on African Affairs, July 24, 1977.

176. Ibid., pp. 350, 354-359; see also discussion on cooperative agreements in George M. Houser, *U.S. Policy and Southern Africa,* The Africa Fund, New York, 1974, pp. 23-24.

177. Immanuel Wallerstein, "Kissinger's African Mischief," *The Nation,* October 9, 1976.

178. Jim Hoagland, *South Africa: Civilization in Conflict* (Boston, Houghton Mifflin, 1972), p. 361. Also Houser, op. cit., p. 5.

179. Hoagland, op. cit., pp. 361-362.

180. Arthur M. Schlesinger, Jr., *A Thousand Days* (Boston, Houghton Mifflin Co., 1965), p. 580.

181. Ibid., p. 581.

182. Hoagland, op. cit., p. 364.

183. Schlesinger, op. cit., p. 583.

184. Steven Talbot, "United States Intervention in Southern Africa: The New Era," *Socialist Revolution,* July-August, 1977, p. 11.

185. National Security Council Memorandum 39, in *The Kissinger Study of Southern Africa,* edited with an introduction by Mohamed A. El-Khawas and Barry Cohen (Westport, Conn., Lawrence Hill & Co.), p. 105.

186. NSSM 39, Ibid., p. 87.

187. In El-Khawas and Cohen, Ibid., quoting Edgar Lockwood, p. 22.

188. NSSM 39, p. 87.

189. NSSM 39, p. 105.

190. NSSM 39, p. 197.

191. NSSM 39, see "Operational Examples," on p. 107.

192. NSSM 39, p. 106.

193. Hoagland, op. cit., p. 365.

194. Ibid. and Talbot, op. cit., p. 13.

195. Talbot, Ibid.

196. Hoagland.

197. An excellent study of the Byrd Amendment appears in El-Khawas and Cohen, op. cit., pp. 40-45.

198. Houser, op. cit., p. 5.

199. Senate Subcommittee on African Affairs, July 23, 1975, p. 315.

200. Quoted by Talbot, op. cit., p. 16, a statement by *New York Times* reporter Seymour Hersch.

201. Henry Kissinger, "United States Policy on Southern Africa," Department of State Bulletin, May 31, 1976.

202. Henry Kissinger, "The Secretary of State, Press Conference," Bureau of Public Affairs, Department of State, September 11, 1976.

203. Kissinger, May 31, 1976.

204. Sean Gervasi and James Turner, CIC Brief, Corporate Information Center, New York, September 1977.

205. Hearing before the Subcommittee on Africa and International Organization of the Committee on International Relations, House of Representatives, February 24, 1977, p. 8.

206. Cyrus Vance, "The Secretary of State, Statement," Bureau of Public Affairs, Department of State, February 10, 1977.

207. Cyrus Vance, "Address to the Plenary Session of the NAACP," Press Release, Department of State, July 1, 1977, p. 11.

208. *Financial Mail* interview, November 5, 1976, House Subcommittee on Africa, March 3, 1977, p. 15.

209. James Morrell and David Gisselquist, "How the IMF Slipped $464 Million to South Africa," Center for International Policy, Washington, D.C., Special Report, January 1978. South Africa's increased military spending came to $450 million in 1976/77, almost the same amount as IMF assistance for that period.

210. The best source of information on Congressional activity is the Washington Office on Africa, 110 Maryland Ave., N.E., Washington, D.C. 20002.

211. George Ball, "Asking for Trouble in South Africa," *Atlantic Monthly*, October, 1977.

212. *The Economist*, November 5, 1977.

213. Ibid.

214. Associated Press, October 27, 1977.

Section Three

1. *South African Perspective*, (The Africa Fund, 1976), p. 1.

2. Ibid., p. 2.

3. Senator Dick Clark, *Africa: Report to the Committee on Foreign Relations, United States Senate*, Washington, D.C., U.S. Govt. Printing Office, July 1977, p. 34.

4. *The Washington Post*, January 14, 1977, p. 12.

5. *The Washington Post*, October 29, 1977.

6. Don K. Morton, *Partners in Apartheid*, Council for Christian Social Action, United Church of Christ, (White Plains, N.Y., Printcraft, 1973), p. 40.

7. *South African Perspectives*, p. 4.

8. Ibid., p. 3.

9. *Johannesburg Star*, November 12, 1977.

10. Morton, op. cit., pp. 39-40.

11. Ibid.

12. *South African Perspectives*, p. 3.

13. *New York Times*, November 6, 1977, Section E.

14. *Washington Post,* October 29, 1977.

15. Ibid.

16. Ibid.

17. *Southern Africa,* Volume XI, No. 3, April 1978.

18. *Johannesburg Star,* November 26, 1977, p. 15.

19. Investor Responsibility Research Center (IRRC), *U.S. Business and South Africa: The Withdrawal Issue,* Special Report 1977-D, November, 1977, p. 34.

20. For white jobless figures for 1976, see *Annual Survey of Race Relations: 1976,* p. 281. For black figures, see estimates of Lieb Loots, researcher in office of Prime Minister's Economic Advisor, *Financial Mail,* March 25, 1977.

21. *Newsweek,* October 3, 1977, p. 46.

22. *Financial Mail,* August 26, 1977, p. 775.

23. Ibid., p. 774.

24. For more information on current anti-apartheid research and activity, contact: South Africa Catalyst Project; American Committee on Africa and Campaign to Oppose Bank Loans to South Africa (305 E. 46 St., New York, New York); Interfaith Center on Corporate Responsibility (475 Riverside Drive, Room 566, New York, New York 10027); American Friends Service Committee (1501 Cherry St., Philadelphia, Pa. 19102); Washington Office on Africa; and Institute for Policy Studies.

A good resource list which includes local groups, appeared in the *Guardian,* (N.Y.C.) Special Supplement on Africa, May 24, 1978.

25. IRRC, op. cit., p. 28.

26. Ibid., pp. 26-27.

27. *The Washington Post,* October 25, 1977.

Appendix I

Partial List of American Firms Operating in South Africa

AAF-International
ABS Worldwide Technical Services, Inc.
Abbott Laboratories
AFIA Worldwide Insurance
Allied Chemical Corporation
Amchem Products Inc.
American Airlines Inc.
American Bureau of Shipping
American Can Company
American Cyanamid Company
American Home Products Corp.
American Hospital Suppy Corp.
American International Group.
American Motors Corporation
Ampex International Operations
Arthur Andersen & Co.
Anderson Clayton & Co.
Applied Power Inc.
Armco Steel Corporation
Automated Building Components Inc.
Avis Incorporated
Ayerst International Inc.
Baxter Laboratories Inc.
Bristol-Myers International Corp.
Batten, Barton, Durstine & Osborn, Inc.
Bechtel Corporation
Bechman Instruments Inc.
Berkshire International Corp.
The Black Clawson
The Black and Decker Manufacturing Co.
Blue Bell Inc.
Boeing International Corporation
Borden Inc.
Borg-Warner Corporation

Buckman Laboratories Inc.
Bucyrus-Erie Company
Bulova Watch Co. Inc.
Bundy Corporation
Burroughs Corporation
Caltex Petroleum Corporation
The Carborundum Company
Carnation International
Cascade Corporation
J.I. Case International
Caterpillar Tractor Company
CBS International
Celanese Corporation
C.G.S. Scientific Corp.
Champion Spark Plug Company
Cheeseborough-Pond's Inc.
The Coca-Cola Export Corporation
Colgate-Palmolive Company
Collier Macmillan International
Computer Sciences Corporation
Chicago Pneumatic Tool Company
Columbus McKinnon Corp.
Control Data Corporation
CPC International Inc.
Crown Cork & Seal Co.
Cutler-Hammer Incorporated
Cyanamid International
Dames & Moore
Dart Industries Inc.
Deere & Company
Del Monte Corporation
Deloitte Haskins & Sells
DeWitt International Corporation
D.H.J. Industries Inc.
Diners Club Inc.
The Diversey Corporation
Dobbs-Life Savers International

Donaldson Company Inc.

The Dow Chemical Company

Dresser Industries Inc.

DuBois International

Dun & Bradstreet Inc.

E.I. Du Pont de Nemours & Co.

Eastman-Kodak Company

The Echlin Manufacturing Company

Encyclopedia Britannica Inc.

Engelhard Minerals & Chemicals Corporation

Envirotech Corporation

Exxon Corporation

J.A. Ewing & McDonald Inc.

Farrell Lines Inc.

Federal-Mogul Corporation

Fiat-Allis Construction Machinery Inc.

Firestone Tire & Rubber Company

FMC Corporation

F & M Systems Company

Ford Motor Company

Fram Corporation

Franklin Electric

Gardner-Denver Company

The Gates Rubber Company

General Electric Company

General Motors Corporation

General Tire and Rubber Company

Geosource Inc.

J. Gerber & Company

Gilbert & Barker Manufacturing Co.

The Gillette Company

The Goodyear Tire & Rubber Company

W.R. Grace & Company

Grolier International Inc.

Hammond Corporation

Heinemann Electric Company

Helena Rubinstein Inc.

Walter E. Heller International Corporation

Heublein International

Hewlett Packard International

Holiday Inn International

Honeywell Inc.

The Hoover Company

Hussman Refrigerators Company

Hydro-Air International Limited

Hyster Company

IBM World Trade Corporation

Ingersoll-Rand Company

Inmont Corporation

Insurance Company of North America

International Flavors & Fragrance Incorporated

International Harvester Company

International Minerals and Chemical Corp.

Interpace Corporation

The Interpublic Group of Companies, Inc.

International Telephone and Telegraph Corporation

Johns-Manville Corp.

Johnson & Johnson

S.C. Johnson & Son Inc.

Joy Manufacturing Company

Kellogg Company

Kelly-Springfield Tire Company

The Kendall Company

Kennecott Copper Corporation

Kidder, Peabody & Co., Inc.

King Resources

Eli Lilly and Company

The Lubrizol Corporation

Lykes Lines Agency Inc.

P.R. Mallory & Co.

Maremont Corporation

Masonite Corporation

Max Factor and Company Inc.

McGraw-Hill International Book Co.

MDS Executive Headquarters

Measurex Corporation

Merck & Co., Inc.

Metro-Goldwyn-Mayer International Inc.

George J. Meyer Manufacturing

Middle West Services Corp.

Miles Laboratories

Mine Safety Appliances Company

Minnesota Mining and Manufacturing Co.

Mobil Oil Corporation

Monsanto Company

Moore-McCormack Lines Inc.

Motorola Inc.

M & T Chemicals Inc.

Muller & Phipps International Corp.

Nabisco, Inc.

Nalco Chemical Corporation

Nashua Corporation

NCR Corporation

National Chemsearch Corporation

National Standard Company

Newmont Mining Corporation

A.C. Nielsen International Inc.

Norton Company

Norton Simon, Inc.

Oak Industries Inc.

Olin Corporation

Oshkosh Truck Corporation

Owens-Corning Fiberglass Corporation

Pacific Oilseeds Inc.

Pan American World Airways, Inc.

Parke, Davis & Company

Parker-Hannifin Corporation

The Parker Pen Company

PepsiCo Inc.

Perkin-Elmer Corporation

Permatex Corporation

Pfizer International Inc.

Phelps Dodge Corporation

Phillips Petroleum Company

Pizza Inn Inc.

Placid Oil Company

International Playtex Inc.

Plough Inc.

Precision Value Corporation

Preformed Line Products Co.

Preload Engineering Corp.

Price Waterhouse & Co.

Ramsey Engineering Company

Rath & Strong Ltd.

Raytheon

Readers Digest Assn. Inc.

Revlon Inc.

Rexnord, Inc.

Rheem International

Richardson-Merrell Inc.

A.H. Robins Co. Inc.

The Robbins Co.

H.H. Roberston Company

Rockwell International Corp.

Rohm and Haas/Philadelphia

Samincorp Inc.

Schering-Plough Corporation

Scholl Inc.

Scripto Incorporated

G.D. Searle Co.

U.S. Shulton Inc.

Simplicity Pattern Co. Inc.

The Singer Company

Smith, Kline & French Laboratories

Sperry Rand Corporation

Standard Brands Inc.

Standard Oil Company of California

Standard Pressed Steel Company

The Stanley Works

Sterling Drug, Inc.

Sterling Products Inc.

Stowe-Woodward Company

Square D Company

E.R. Squibb & Sons Inc.

Sybrnon Corporation

Tampax Inc.

Tanatex Chemical Corporation

Taylor Instrument Companies

Technicon Corporation

Tenneco International Inc.

Texaco Inc.
Texasgulf Inc.
The Timken Company

Titan Industrial Corporation
Tokheim Corporation
The Trane Company
TransWorld Airlines Inc.
TRW Inc.
20th Century-Fox Films Corp.
Twin Disc Incorporated
Union Carbide Corp.
Uniroyal Inc.
United Artists Corp.
United States Filter Corp.
United States Gypsum Co.
United States Industries

United States Steel Corporation
The Upjohn Company
Valvoline Oil Company
The Valeron Corporation
Van Dusen Air Incorporated
Warner Bros. Inc.
Warner-Lambert Company
Western Airlines Inc.
Westinghouse Electric Corp.
West Point Pepperell Inc.
Whinney Murray Ernst and Ernst
White Motor Corporation
Wilbur-Ellis Company
Wyeth International Limited
Xerox Corporation
Arthur Young & Company

Appendix II

Bank Loans to South Africa*

American Express International Banking Corp.
American National Bank & Trust Co. (Chicago)
The Arizona Bank
Bank of America
Bank of Boston International
Bank of New York
Bankers Trust New York Corp.
Central Cleveland International Bank
Central Merchant Bank
Central National Bank of Chicago
Central National Bank of Cleveland
Chartered Bank
Chase Manhattan
Chemical Bank (New York)
Citibank (New York)
Citibank International (Chicago)
Citizens & Southern National Bank (Atlanta)
City National Bank of Detroit
Cleveland Trust Co.
Continental Bank International (Houston)
Continental Bank International (New York)
Continental Illinois
Crocker Bank International (Chicago)
Crocker National Bank (Los Angeles, San Francisco)
European American Banking Corp.
European American Bank & Trust Co.
Fidelity International Bank (New York)
First Boston Corp.
First Chicago Corp.
First City National Bank (Houston)
First National Bank of Atlanta
First National Bank of Boston

---

*This list of banks, that have made loans to South Africa or to U.S. companies for activities in South Africa, is based on *U.S. Bank Loans to South Africa* by the Corporate Data Exchange, Inc. (CDE). CDE's study is the most comprehensive to date and is available for $3.00 from Corporate Data Exchange, Room 707, 198 Broadway, New York, N.Y. 10038, (212) 962-2980. It provides information on parent companies and foreign banks and can be purchased at bulk rates.

First National Bank of Chicago
First National Bank (Dallas)
First National Bank (Louisville)
First National Bank of Minneapolis
First National Citibank International (Los Angeles)
First Pennsylvania Bank NA
First Wisconsin National Bank of Milwaukee
French Bank of California
Harris Bank International Corp. (New York)
Harris Trust & Savings Bank (Chicago)
Houston National Bank
Huntington National Bank (Columbus, Ohio)
Irving Trust Co. (New York)
Manufacturers Hanover (New York)
Manufacturers & Traders Trust Co.
Marine Midland Bank (Buffalo)
Maryland National Bank
Mellon Bank International (New York)
Mellon Bank NA (Pittsburgh)
Merchants National Bank (Cedar Rapids, Iowa)
Merchants National Bank & Trust Co. (Indianapolis)
Morgan Guaranty Trust Co. (New York)
National Citybank (Cleveland)
National Bank of Detroit
New Jersey Bank NA (Paterson)
North Carolina National Bank
Northern Trust Bank
Northern Trust International Banking Co. (New York)
Northwestern National Bank of Minneapolis
Northwestern National Bank (Omaha)
Philadelphia International Bank (New York)
Philadelphia National Bank
Pittsburgh National Bank
Provident National Bank (Philadephia)
Republic National Bank of Dallas
Security Pacific National Bank
Society National Bank of Cleveland
Trust Company of Georgia (Atlanta)
United California Bank International
United Virginia Bank
Wells Fargo Bank (Los Angeles, San Francisco)
Winters National Bank & Trust Co. (Dayton)

Investment Banks

Blyth Eastman Dillon & Co.
Brown Bros Harriman & Co.
Dean Witter Reynolds Org.
Dillon Read & Co. Inc.
First Boston Inc.
Goldman Sachs & Co.
Kidder Peabody & Co. Inc.
Lazard Freres & Co.
Lehman Brothers Inc.
Loeb Rhoades & Co.
Merrill Lynch & Co. Inc.
Morgan Stanley & Co. Inc.
Paine Webber Inc.
Salomon Brothers
Smith Barney Harris Upham & Co. Inc.

IPS Publications

Black South Africa Explodes
By Counter Information Services

The only detailed account available of events in South Africa in the first year since the uprising which began in June 1976 in Soweto. The report exposes the reality of life in the African townships, the impact of South Africa's economic crisis on blacks, and the white regime's dependence on European and American finance. $2.95.

Buying Time in South Africa
By Counter Information Services

An update of events in South Africa since 1976. Despite a severe recession, continuing struggle and external criticism, the South Africa state has reaffirmed and increased its control. Supported by world banks, multinationals and governments with an economic stake in South Africa, the racist regime is implementing the "grand apartheid" by eliminating all blacks through the creation of home states. $2.95.

The Sullivan Principles:
Decoding Corporate Camouflage
By Elizabeth Schmidt

An analysis of the Sullivan Principles, the fair employment code devised by American corporations in South Africa to deflect public criticism of investment in that country. Demonstrates that even corporations pledged to these principles inevitably bolster the white minority regime with capital, technology and know-how. $1.50.

The Political Economy of Race and Class in South Africa
By Bernard Makhosezwe Magubane

An historical analysis of the interrelationship between race and class in the context of South African development. Addressing the displacement of the indigenous Africans, the migrant-labor system and the development of "native reserves," this examination of the current crisis concludes with a discussion of the growing opposition movement. $18.50.

The State and Revolution in East Africa
By John S. Saul

This incisive study identifies external control and internal inequality as obstacles to progress in the countries of Eastern Africa—Tanzania, Uganda and Kenya. Linking revolutionary endeavors in Mozambique to the struggle in South Africa, this work examines the nature of the post-colonial state, the dynamics of politics, the significance of tribalism, and the revolutionary potential of workers and peasants. $16.50.

South Africa and the United States: An Annotated Bibliography
By Kevin Danaher

This convenient reference manual lists 221 books and articles on U.S. involvement in South Africa. Citations present standard bibliographic information and a brief description of the work. Includes map, index, and addresses of other resource organizations and liberation movement offices in the U.S. $3.00.

Race & Class

The quarterly journal of the Institute for Race Relations and the Transnational Institute. Articles examine the liberation movements of Africa and Asia, emerging state structures and ideology. Features also include book reviews, studies of Third World literature, the problems of women, workers and peasants. Subscriptions: $7.00 individuals; $15.00 institutions.

The Politics of National Security
By Marcus G. Raskin

This historical analysis of the national security state traces its evolution from a planning instrument to ensure national stability, mute class conflicts and secure the domestic economy to the basis for covert and overt imperialism. The debacle in Indochina, the genocidal nature of the arms race, and growing economic instability, however, signal the decline of this structure. This incisive study impels renewed public debate of national policy and purpose. $5.95.

Peace in Search of Makers
Riverside Church Reverse the Arms Race Convocation
Jane Rockman, Editor

A compilation of papers denouncing the proliferation of sophisticated weaponry, which threatens a nuclear cataclysm and destroys our society by diverting resources from social services and programs. This volume confronts the moral, economic, strategic and ethical aspects of the arms race and appeals for a citizen coalition to reverse the course of social decay and uncontrolled nuclear armament. Contributions by Richard Barnet, Michael Klare, Cynthia Arnson, Marcus Raskin and others. $5.95.

The Counterforce Syndrome:
A Guide to U.S. Nuclear Weapons and Strategic Doctrine
By Robert C. Aldridge

An identification of how "counterforce" has replaced "deterrence" as the Pentagon's prevailing doctrine, contrary to what most Americans believe. This thorough summary and analysis of U.S. strategic nuclear weapons and military doctrine includes descriptions of MIRVs, MARVs, Trident systems, cruise missiles, and M-X missiles as they relate to the aims of a U.S. first strike. $3.95.

The Giants
Russia and America
By Richard Barnet

An authoritative, comprehensive account of the latest stage of the complex U.S.-Soviet relationship; how it came about, what has changed, and where it is headed.

"A thoughtful and balanced account of American-Soviet relations. Barnet goes beyond current controversies to discuss the underlying challenges of a relationship that is crucial to world order." — Cyril E. Black, Director, Center for International Studies, Princeton University

"An extraordinarily useful contribution to the enlightenment of the people of this country . . . . It is of fundamental importance that we understand the true state of our relations with Russia if we are to avoid a tragic mistake in our future." — Senator J.W. Fulbright. $3.95.

Dubious Specter:
A Second Look at the 'Soviet Threat'
By Fred Kaplan

A thorough exposition and analysis of the myths and realities surrounding the current U.S.-Soviet "military balance." Kaplan's comparisons of U.S. and Soviet nuclear arsenals and strategies provide the necessary background for understanding current debates on arms limitations and rising military costs. $2.95.

The Rise and Fall of the 'Soviet Threat':
Domestic Sources of the Cold War Consensus
By Alan Wolfe

A timely essay which demonstrates that American fear of the Soviet Union tends to fluctuate due to domestic factors, not in relation to the military and foreign policies of the USSR. Wolfe contends that recurring features of American domestic politics periodically coalesce to spur anti-Soviet sentiment, contributing to increased tensions and dangerous confrontations. $3.95.

Resurgent Militarism
By Michael T. Klare
and the Bay Area Chapter
of the Inter-University Committee

An analysis of the origins and consequences of the growing militaristic fervor which is spreading from Washington across the nation. The study examines America's changing strategic position since Vietnam and the political and economic forces which underlie the new upsurge in militarism. $2.00.

Toward World Security:
A Program for Disarmament
By Earl C. Ravenal

This proposal argues that in light of destabilizing new strategic weapons systems and increasing regional conflicts which could involve the superpowers, the U.S. should take independent steps toward disarmament by not deploying new "counterforce" weapons, pledging no first use of nuclear weapons, and by following a non-interventionist foreign policy. $2.00.

Conventional Arms Restraint:
An Unfulfilled Promise
By Michael T. Klare and Max Holland

A review of several aspects of current steps to reduce the amounts and sophistication of weapons sold, close loopholes in Carter administration policy on overall sales, especially to human rights violators, reduce secrecy, improve Congressional oversight, limit co-production arrangements and restrict sales of police and related equipment to authoritarian regimes abroad. $2.00.

Myths and Realities
of the 'Soviet Threat'
Proceedings of an IPS Conference on U.S.-Soviet Relations

Distinguished experts explore the prospect for change in the USSR, define the role of the Soviet military in Eastern Europe and assess the U.S.-Soviet military balance. Based on reliable data and analytical rigor, these statements debunk the myth of a new Soviet threat. $2.00.

The New Generation of Nuclear Weapons
By Stephen Daggett

An updated summary of strategic weapons, including American and Soviet nuclear hardware. These precarious new technologies may provoke startling shifts in strategic policy, leading planners to consider fighting "limited nuclear wars" or consider a preemptive first strike capability. $.75.

Supplying Repression:
U.S. Support for Authoritarian Regimes Abroad
By Michael T. Klare

A description of how the U.S. continues to supply arms and training to police and other internal security forces of repressive governments abroad. "Very important, fully documented indictment of U.S. role in supplying rightist Third World governments with the weaponry and know-how of repression." — *The Nation.* $2.95.

The Nuclear Disaster
By Counter Information Services

An analysis of Great Britain's nuclear power industry. A history of government mismanagement, secrecy and subsidized profits for private energy monopolies is contrasted with the dismal record of the nuclear power industry regarding escalating prices, declining job creation, and health dangers from radiation and nuclear waste disposal. An appendix profiling nuclear companies, state regulating agencies, U.K. reactor orders, and a chronology of nuclear power is included. $2.95.

The Ford Report
By Counter Information Services

This "anti-report" by CIS, a London affiliate of the Institute for Policy Studies, is a comprehensive and well-documented study on the Ford Motor Company. The report deals with Ford activities in South Africa, its role in the Common Market, its plans for the Third World, wages and working conditions, death on the job, profits and production, and Ford's blueprint for the future. $2.95.

The New Technology
By Counter Information Services

This report investigates the effects of new technology. Examining the current revolution in microelectronics, the survey demonstrates that while electronic "chips" could eliminate tedious jobs, reduce work time and enhance the quality of life for millions, the resulting efficiency will increase unemployment and shift remaining jobs to unskilled work forces. $2.95.

The New Gnomes:
Multinational Banks in the Third World
By Howard M. Wachtel

This work documents and analyzes the growth of Third World debt to private U.S.-based multinational banks, and the impact of this new form of indebtedness on the politics and economic policies of Third World countries. $3.95.

Chile:
Economic 'Freedom' and Political Repression
By Orlando Letelier

A dramatic analysis by the former leading official of the Allende government who was assassinated by the Pinochet junta. This essay demonstrates the necessary relationship between an economic development model which benefits only the wealthy few and the political terror which has reigned in Chile since the overthrow of the Allende regime. $1.00.

Human Rights, Economic Aid and Private Banks:
The Case of Chile
By Michael Moffitt and Isabel Letelier

This issue paper documents the tremendous increase in private bank loans to the Chilean military dictatorship since the overthrow of Salvador Allende in 1973. Previously unpublished data demonstrates how private banks rescued the Chilean military government by increasing loans to Chile at the very time governments and international institutions were reducing their loans because of massive human rights violations. $2.00.

The Links Between Struggles for Human Rights
in the United States and the Third World
By Congressman Ron Dellums

The keynote address at the 1978 Letelier-Moffitt Human Rights Memorial. Stating that human rights violations stem from the system, not the individual, he calls for a powerful coalition of all minorities, Third World people and progressive human beings to change America and the world. $.50.

The First Americans:
Fighting for a Future to Inherit the Past
By Pablo Letelier and Judy L. Ziegler

An account of the Mapuche's struggle against the policies which threaten the extinction of all indigenous groups in Chile. This indictment of the Chilean military regime is the first in a series designed to document the historical and current exploitation and human rights violations of Native Americans. $1.95.

Whistle-Blowers Guide
to the Federal Bureaucracy
By Government Accountability Project

This handbook was written to aid employees of the federal government who need to reach the public with evidence of illegal or improper practices in their agencies. Based on the experience of such veterans as Ernie Fitzgerald, it tells prospective whistleblowers the consequences to expect and how to afford themselves maximum protection. $3.00.

Public Employee Pension Funds: New Strategies for Investment
By Lee Webb and William Schweke

A guide detailing channels for redirecting public pension fund assets to socially useful investments. This work surveys legal questions, portfolio management, political and institutional obstacles and alternative investment opportunities. Including a bibliography and glossary of financial terms, this volume is essential for public officials and employee unions, economic development specialists and public interest groups. $9.95/$14.95 institutions.

Tax Abatements: Resources for Public Officials and Community Leaders
By Ed Kelly and Lee Webb

A current examination of tax abatements which favor corporations with special deals while increasing onerous local property taxes. Attributing the problem to corporate influence on local government, this analysis identifies the tactics successfully employed by public officials, community groups and labor unions to thwart corporate parasitism. $4.95/$6.95 institutions.

Plant Closings: Resources for Public Officials and Community Leaders
Ed Kelly and Lee Webb, Editors

A comprehensive resource manual detailing the problems of plant closings and runaway shops. This collection of essays, magazine articles, policy reports and press clips outlines the causes of plant closings and prescribes organizing and legislative strategies to prevent them. Indispensible for union leaders, public officials, academics and community activists. $4.95/$6.95 institutions.

State and Local Tax Reform Perspective, Proposal and Resources
Dean Tipps and Lee Webb, Editors

A comprehensive guide to state and local tax issues. Progressive tax experts discuss both the problems of tax equity and the prospects for reform initiatives, emphasizing property, estate and sales taxes and innovative proposals for taxing land speculation, business and corporate profits. This compendium includes original articles, material from periodicals, leaflets, and memos prepared in tax reform campaigns. $9.95/$14.95 institutions.

Public Policy for the 80's:
Perspectives and Resources
for State and Local Action
Lee Webb, Editor

The definitive guide to public policy issues for the 80's. This handbook offers rigorous analysis of controversies in energy, economic development, state and local tax reform and agriculture. Focusing on 27 critical issues facing state and local governments, nationally recognized experts present extensive resource information on organizations, individuals and publications for policymaking in the 80's. $9.95/$14.95 institutions.

The Public Balance Sheet:
A New Tool for Evaluating Economic Choices

This useful paper introduces an innovative conceptual tool for assessing the impact of public and private economic decisions. Clarifying policy choices in terms of their implications for the community, "the public balance sheet" offers public officials and policy analysts a comprehensive approach to economic planning and fiscal responsibility. $2.95/$4.95 for institutions.

Industrial Exodus
By Ed Kelly

A classic study of strategies for preventing plant closings and run-away shops. Outlining a program for unions, community groups, states and the federal government, this concise manual is widely used by labor and local organizations to save jobs and protect communities from plant shutdown. $2.95/$4.95 institutions.

Postage and Handling:
All orders must be prepaid. For delivery within the USA, please add 15% of order total. For delivery outside the USA, add 20%. Standard discounts available upon request.

Please write the Institute for Policy Studies, 1901 Que Street, N.W., Washington, D.C. 20009 for our complete catalog of publications and films.